Walk With Me

Revealing One Man's Faith

BY PHILLIP HIGHTOWER

Copyright © 2014 by Phillip Hightower

Walk With Me
Revealing One Man's Faith
by Phillip Hightower

Printed in the United States of America

ISBN 9781628718195

All rights reserved solely by the author. The author guarantees all contents are original and do not infringe upon the legal rights of any other person or work. No part of this book may be reproduced in any form without the permission of the author. The views expressed in this book are not necessarily those of the publisher.

Unless otherwise indicated, Bible quotations are taken from Holy Bible, New International Version®, NIV® copyright © 1973, 1978, 1984, 2011 by Biblica, Inc. and the King James Version (KJV) by Public Domain

www.xulonpress.com

*For Tonia, Aaron, and Kaylie.
God, I want to live my life to see you smile.*

TABLE OF CONTENTS

Foreword: ix
Chapter I: Spiders and Thrones 13
Chapter II: Seeing is not Believing 21
Chapter III: Black Lake Converts 29
Chapter IV: A Cardboard Fort 37
Chapter V: Hazmat Honeymoon 46
Chapter VI: Gone Not Forgotten 54
Chapter VII: Meeting at the Stump 64
Chapter VIII: Liftoff. 73
Chapter IX: What Could Possibly Go Wrong 81
Chapter X: Flaming Ice Picks 90
Chapter XI: Dumpster Dog 99
Chapter XII: Dating Anxiety 108
Chapter XIII: Lisa and the Library 116
Chapter XIV: Here In This Moment 124
Chapter XV: Chewing Tobacco 132
Chapter XVI: Perfect 140
Epilogue: 148
About me: 151

Foreword:

Gathering and processing details of health records is a regular part of my job. Sadly, the routine can be twice as boring as it sounds, but it does require a great deal of concentration. Focusing on the tasks at hand one particular day was different.

That day I found my mind going over all the encouragement that I'd been receiving about writing. Sometimes we discount the encouragement of others as just an attempt on their part to be friendly and perhaps sometimes that is all that it is. Then sometimes there is just too much encouragement for it to be counted as anything less than God.

Thoughts that my devotional work wasn't good enough to share were that morning being met with the thoughts that they needed to be. Individual encouragements were collectively bringing me to a point that I hadn't been before: the idea that I was meant to write something that would make a difference for the kingdom.

Normally I would dismiss such thoughts as sort of delusions of grandeur that something I could do might make an impact, but this day was different. My focus was drawn away from my work to the idea that putting together my devotions could be something that would please the Lord.

At some point through the course of the day, I mentioned to my wife what was going on in my mind. I was thinking about putting some of the things I'd written together and unlike other days, the idea of it was making it difficult for me to concentrate on my work. It excited me.

I managed to get my day behind me and I'd pushed what then felt like daydreams aside. Routinely I stop at my mailbox in the afternoons before going on to the house. On top of the small pile of mail inside the box was an advertising postcard. There was my burning bush, my light on the way to Damascus. In large letters, the first line of text on the back of it read, "Publish your book."

Foreword:

I'm not doing this in the expectation of becoming a renowned author or to be counted among great theologians. I just want to move in obedience. It isn't everyday you get a postcard from God!

My goals in writing this are to encourage faith in others and to grow my own faith by moving in what I believe the Lord would have me do. It's a collection of personal stories and observations meant to make you think, examine your hope, and laugh.

The faith of some people seems to say, "Too bad you can't go where I'm going," or "I'm glad I'm His favorite." I want a faith that says, "Brother, come go with me," and "Let grace abound, because without it, I'd be lost." Being a Christian doesn't make us perfect, but draws us to a place where God can work His perfection in us.

Although...if God doesn't have a sense of humor, then I'm in serious trouble.

Chapter I

SPIDERS AND THRONES

When I was sixteen, I felt good about myself. High school friends seemed so close and the future was a place I was anxious to go. My folks built my self esteem high, while seeing to it that I never looked down on anyone else. I knew I needed God's grace for where I fell short and I sought it. Everything seemed okay.

Then a shadow fell across my life. No matter how hard I tried, there were thoughts that I could not put down. Despair is like a bottomless pit. You can fall so far down that without help eventually you don't remember which way is up. That's where I found myself. In the beginning, no one close to me had experienced anything like it, so they didn't know how to help.

What should have been some of the best years of my high school days turned into a nightmare. I withdrew a lot from family and friends, although I managed to put on a bold face. Behaving the way I was expected became harder and harder, because inside I was tormented. Thin and without endurance, my heart raced constantly, and I began to have tremors. Although the onset was slow, I was becoming horribly sick.

Lying on an examination table, I'd reached a critical moment. A small town doctor took a look at me and made an immediate diagnosis. I had severe Graves' disease. Graves' disease is the name given to a collection of symptoms caused from an overactive thyroid gland. It was rare in men, rarer still in one my age, but mine was on fire.

The diagnosis began a physical recovery process that culminated in serious surgery with the removal of the thyroid gland, but because my hormone levels had been so high for so long there was tissue damage behind my eyes that scarred them, causing them to protrude slightly. Worse than any tissue damage, the landscape of my mind looked like a battlefield with no victors.

Where was God? It's human nature to wonder. God was there in the love of my parents. God was there when I asked forgiveness and did not deserve it. God was there arranging things to help me when I was falling into despair and no one else knew how to help. God was there at the exam table and the operating room having orchestrated those moments. God was there to bind wounds on that battlefield where he knew a survivor lay. God was there wanting me to come closer.

I did not realize all of this when I was going through it, but I believe he is laboring with me now to see things through the faith that I claim. He never wanted me to be sick. He wanted me to have hope and a future, and the clearer my vision of him, the greater those things have become. "I have told you these things, so that in me you may have peace. In this world you will have trouble. But take heart! I have overcome the world." (John 16:33 NIV)

- Personal change. It's something that I've been praying for a long time. If God were not God, I think sometimes he would roll his eyes when I begin to ask again about something with which I struggle. We want what we want, and we want it yesterday. Don't make me deal with me. Just zap me, God, and fix it! Ever felt that way?

I firmly believe God could hit my reset button, but he doesn't force people to change. I could make my children do what I say by punishing them and pushing them into everything, but their hearts would only be further away. If it were somehow possible to replace them with copies that only did exactly as I predetermined, they would be empty and cold. He wants real love from us. How does he do it?

Once we accept the truth of the word, and place ourselves at the foot of the cross, he begins to correct our perception. We're covered by grace from the moment we invite Jesus into our lives as Lord and Savior, but our transformation into who he would have us be is day by day. He delights when we seek him! If he demanded our perfection before we approached him, then no one would have a chance.

I'm not completely the person that I need to be, but I hope that you will listen when I tell you this: Jesus is life. If you've already received him, ask him to draw you closer. If you've never received him, ask for forgiveness and invite him into your heart!

- If you're a fault finder, let me save you the trouble. There is no halo around my head, and my feet do not float above the ground. If you knew me, you'd know I've made my share of mistakes, and I don't pretend otherwise. Visit my social network page, and I'm sure you'd find something that would raise an eyebrow.

I'm not one with the universe, struggle with myself on a daily basis, and wonder why some things had to be as they are. Probably just like you.

So, what can I speak of that I believe can make a difference in your life that makes a difference in my own? Faith. Not in me. Not in a cause. Not in religion. Only in Jesus.

Reality. Jesus was the embodiment of God on the earth. He paid the price of your sins, and it was personal. He wanted you to know how much he loves you, and he died to prove it. The grave could not keep him, and he offers you new and everlasting life.

After showing himself to Thomas who wanted to see the risen Lord with his own eyes, Jesus said, "Because you have seen me, you have believed. Blessed are those who have not seen and yet have believed." (partial John 20:29 NIV) You do not have to have physical proof to have saving faith. You have to choose to accept him.

God rewards those who earnestly want him, and he is available to you in this moment. The haughty won't receive his favor, but he will hear a repentant heart. Ask him to increase your faith!

- Peter didn't think they would catch anything. He and his friends had fished all night with no success. Still, when Jesus, who had been using Peter's boat to speak to the crowd that had gathered there, asked him to try his nets again, he obeyed. Despite every empty net before, when he drew them up, this time they were full to the point of breaking. "When Simon Peter saw this, he fell at Jesus' knees and said, 'Go away from me, Lord. I am a sinful man!'" (Luke 5:8 NIV) As Peter began to have a greater realization of who Jesus was, that same realization was illuminating the nature of his own heart.

Just as with Peter, the closer we draw to God the greater our awareness of our shortcomings. The clearer we see Jesus, the clearer we see ourselves. Peter knew he wasn't worthy, and offered that the Lord depart from him, feeling it was no less than he deserved. Jesus responded, "Don't be afraid..." (partial Luke 5:10 NIV)

Jesus saw everything Peter was feeling, knowing him to the core, but he wanted to stay with him. Peter's confession was a place from which the Lord could begin to work change. Jesus did not want him to be afraid, and he docsn't want you to bc afraid cithcr. Just givc him a place to begin.

- Have you asked for forgiveness? Letting go of guilt may take time, but remember that the debt to your soul was paid for you. God does not ask that we punish ourselves, only that we be sorry for our sins with a willingness to turn from them. We can't move forward in new life if we're self loathing. God wants you to be happy!

Depend on his word for your assurance, "If we confess our sins, He is faithful and just to forgive us our sins and to cleanse us from all unrighteousness." (1 John 1:9 NKJV)

> - "The spider skillfully grasps with its hands, and it is in kings' palaces." (Proverbs 30:28 NKJV)

I was getting settled in to a call of nature, and I was thinking the business might take more than a minute, so I leaned over to pick up the latest Sportsman's Guide catalog when I heard a "tink" sound from the overhead vent. The spinning blades had hit something.

I knew it couldn't be good when I felt something tickle the top of my head, that rolled off in front of me. Staring back at me with eight eyes was a giant spider being cradled gently in my underwear. Okay, maybe it wasn't giant, but when there's a spider in your shorts does the size really matter?

Now, I don't have an unnatural fear of spiders, but I will go ninja if one gets on me. The only trouble is that even the best ninja is pretty much rendered powerless when his pants are around his ankles. My memory gets a little fuzzy after that. Somehow I managed to rip off some paper and grab the tarantula, hurl it in the toilet, and send it on to goldfish heaven.

Talk about spoiling the mood–it took a little while before nature relaxed enough to finish that job.

Chapter II

SEEING IS NOT BELIEVING

You can't judge a book by its cover. This old adage about books came from a time when books did not have graphic covers. These days, often you can know something of a book by its cover. You don't pick up a book with a trashy romance dust jacket and expect to open it up to a history lesson. In the same way, a person willing for their lives to take on the appearance of the sins around them, probably have those same sins hurting their lives.

God is not concerned with the outward appearance and judges the heart (1 Samuel 16:7), so, no, he isn't concerned your haircut or your nose ring. However, a tree is known by its fruit (Luke 6:44), and while people are neither books nor trees, the point is that we adorn our lives from what is within and produce based on what we truly are. What do others see when they look at your life?

• Our culture teaches, follow your heart wherever it leads. It sounds great, because we all want to satisfy our desires. It's natural.

The trouble is without God our hearts are a chaotic place. One minute they're beautiful, flowing with everything held as noble among men. The next minute that beauty is flowing into a sewer, where we find ourselves wallowing in selfishness.

Inviting the Spirit to lead us where our hearts fail is when we begin to align ourselves with what is best for our lives. Follow your heart when it is leading you toward what you believe Jesus would have of you, and don't let your desires take you where favor in his love can't be found.

• We were about to go on vacation, but we discovered the car needed two outer tie rods and bearings replaced. That's was a pretty serious number of paper presidents at this house, and the timing couldn't have been worse. I didn't start shouting, "Hallelujah," and I didn't feel warm and fuzzy about it, but I didn't start swearing and take it out on the world either.

There was a time in my life when I leaned toward the latter, but I've learned being that way only makes bad things worse.

The sound of any complaint I might have been tempted to voice was pathetic compared to the symphony of blessings that I've been given. Material blessings aside, intangible blessings I've received go beyond price. We delude ourselves when we place money at the center of our lives, where it steals our joy and obscures our vision of the truth.

God knows when money is necessary. After all, He is the original realist, but money can't satisfy our greatest need or provide lasting joy. Jesus is my treasure, "For where your treasure is, there will your heart be also." (Matthew 6:21 KJV)

As I considered these things, it did not change the fact that the car needed repairs, but it did correct my perspective. I may not have started with praise, but I could finish with it.

- We build towers in our lives made of the blessings of God, fashioning walls from the apparent security of our health, homes, and financial prosperity. Thinking ourselves safe, we put our lives behind them because the walls seem trustworthy, but how quickly things can change!

Illness strikes us in our mortality. Homes are broken by unfaithful spouses. Jobs are lost. When we've built our defenses from the blessings of God and not God himself, that's when the Enemy comes saying, "If God loved you, then you would not be sick. If God really cared, then he would have kept your home together. If God was real, then you would not stand to lose everything." It's at these times that we should submit ourselves to God and resist those bitter thoughts. The Enemy will flee. (see James 4:7)

God loves you with the same love that brought Jesus from heaven to die on the cross, and that is where our faith should be rooted. He will surely bless us because he loves us, but our faith should be stronger than the presence or absence of blessings. (see Matthew 6:33)

Let Jesus be your tower! "From the ends of the earth I call to you, I call as my heart grows faint. Lead me to the rock that is higher than I. For you have been my refuge, a strong tower against the foe." (Psalm 61:2-3 NIV)

- I'd been praying about old regrets. Who hasn't wished they could fix something in their past?

One night, I dreamed I received a phone call from daddy who has been gone for years now. I knew he went to the grave, yet I knew it was him on the phone. He realized that I thought he was gone, and he wanted to set me straight. He was very much alive. I wasn't afraid, and he wasn't angry about the things in our past that were bothering me.

It was only a dream, but I brought something away from it. I'm reminded that death is as much a beginning as an ending. There will come a day when all the dead in Christ are reunited as the living children of God. "Behold, I tell you a mystery: We shall not all sleep, but we shall all be changed in a moment, in the twinkling of an eye, at the last trumpet. For the trumpet will sound, and the dead will be raised incorruptible, and we shall be changed." (1 Cor 15:51-52 NKJV)

We don't have to be bound by sorrow, because of our promise for tomorrow.

- While vacationing, my son sampled some salsa rightly named, "Death by Salsa." Everyone was watching his reaction to the ridiculously hot stuff. I could see streaks of red fanning out from his ears as he stood there taking the pain. Finally, the salesclerk suggested milk that they carried for that purpose. Setting the carton on the counter, the cashier said that the samples were free, but the milk was four hundred dollars.

Sin is like that salsa. It looks good, everyone in the world wants to see you try it, but in the end there is a price you can't afford to pay.

> "For the wages of sin is death, but the gift of God is eternal life in Christ Jesus our Lord." (Romans 6:23 NKJV)

The cashier was only teasing, of course, but the Devil isn't. He wants to see you in agony and burdened with the mistakes you've made. He'll make sure there are plenty of "free" samples around for you to try.

The good news is if you call on Jesus, you can be saved! (See Romans 10:13)

What can I say? Like father, like son. I remember drinking hot salsa on a bet once.

Seeing is not Believing

- We all understand the phrase, "Seeing is believing." No matter how incredible or unlikely something may be, if we see it for ourselves, then we accept it. It works fine for a lot of things that we encounter, but not for everything.

When an entertaining magician does an act before our eyes, do we believe what he has done is real? Knowing he is a performer, we view what he is doing as a trick even though it seems real because of who we take him to be.

What about things that can't be seen? We use electricity everyday, and if everything is working as it should be, sparks don't fly when we turn on an appliance, but we know electricity is there because of the results. I wonder how many saw the miracles of Christ that did not believe.

Once, Jesus was in the synagogue and a man with a shriveled hand was there. The Jewish leaders wondered if he would heal the man. They knew the man and the problem with his hand. They knew power had come from Jesus before, and anticipated that he might heal him. Jesus healed the man before their eyes, they saw, but they did not believe. They could not deny the man's restored hand, but they denied the Savior because he threatened the way they wanted things to be. (see Mark 3:1-6)

For people, seeing never truly equals believing. Rather, we filter our perceptions through what we choose to hold as truth.

The Spirit of God changes the lives of people. Just like electricity, you may not see it flow, but you can see the results. Peace, hope, and love are available to you.

You do not have to see miracles to believe Jesus for his saving grace, but you must make a choice. Will you live as a believer and be happy over the recorded witness of miracles, or will you reject him because he threatens the way that you think is better?

Seek forgiveness of your sins, and bring your questions, doubts, fears, and struggles to God through prayer. Jesus said, "I am the way and the truth and the life. No one comes to the Father except through me." (partial John 14:6) The way to salvation of your soul is only possible through the blood Jesus shed at the cross. He is the truth you need to know to receive it. Our life is the life he gives.

Chapter III

Black Lake Converts

We made it to Hot Springs the Friday evening of Labor Day weekend. Scattered thunderstorms remained in the area as the result of the weather pattern brought in by hurricane Isaac. Not content to sit at the hotel, my wife and I decided to defy the radar images that we knew were popping up all around us. Killing a little time driving around town satisfied our restlessness but being tired from the trip, we were soon ready to go back to the hotel.

I'm a very careful driver, but my wife might tell you that it is to a fault. Usually, I'm the one behind the wheel when we're together to avoid loving marital discussions of what I perceive as her deficiencies. A font reserved for sarcasm would have been quite useful just now, but the truth be told, I like to be in charge of driving.

As we began our way back, the bottom fell out. A sudden gullywasher so intense for a few moments that the windshield wipers, headlights, streetlights, and reflectors on the road were all for nothing–I couldn't see. I was moving down the road, but I wasn't in control. Slowing down to a snail's pace I was able to reorient myself in the road. I'd traveled well into another lane, so thankfully there were few other cars on the road and none nearby at that time.

Then realization hit me, reminding me, taking the place of the accident that had been avoided. Our best efforts and intentions can't take the place of God's control in our lives. There will be times that we simply are not enough. Alone, we are not equipped to handle everything that we encounter traveling life's road. We must be dependent on God, or come up short. "God is our refuge and strength, a very present help in trouble." (Psalm 46:1 KJV)

"Do you want me to drive?" came the inevitable question from the passenger's side.

"No, definitely not," thinking maybe driving into Lake Hamilton would at least spare myself some embarrassment.

I'm looking to the Lord for his control, but I just wasn't ready for my wife to take the wheel.

- Sometimes when I am alone and my mind is focused on Jesus, a feeling that is difficult to describe immerses me. It's like being brokenhearted and simultaneously being put back together. I'm not who I was the day before and not yet who I'm going to be, but God is working on me.

You don't have to read your Bible twelve hours a day and pray the other twelve. Just make a daily conscious effort welcoming him in the garden of your soul.

Are the pathways blocked? Have animals overrun it? Do weeds choke the flowers? He will tend to you, but you've got to meet in the garden.

Make time for him while there is time. You are not promised tomorrow, and just like our own lives, this world's days are dwindling.

- Life happens. Hopefully, faith isn't an afterthought for us when it does. Faith isn't denial of reality. When we are sick or hurt, then we are sick or hurt. When something breaks our hearts, then they are broken. But we belong to a caring God who knows our pain!

He does not desert us in our need. Circumstances come to us all that are going to impact our immediate attention, but how happy we are in our lives greatly depends on our focus. The place our minds come to rest is where our hearts tend to follow.

> "Finally, brothers and sisters, whatever is true, whatever is noble, whatever is right, whatever is pure, whatever is lovely, whatever is admirable, if anything is excellent or praiseworthy, think about such things." (Phil 4:8 NIV)

Would you be unashamed to meet Jesus where your mind comes to rest?

- Visiting family in New Orleans, no less than three times did I hear young people cursing in public. The first two weren't angry. They weren't in pain. It was as if the words were just a normal part of expression. Not words that were simply impolite for certain social situations. Curses. Words that cross boundaries you can feel.

I'm not saying that when I was young that I never cursed. I'm not saying that I'll never slip when I bash my thumb with a hammer. But I will say that I exercised restraint as a youth because it was taught to me. You didn't swear in public like it was commonplace. My parents would have thinned the seat of my pants with a belt had they ever discovered I'd been disrespecting everyone around me in the way those kids were. Thank God! Now I know that reverence is serving me.

Then there was the third one who wasn't simply speaking them among his friends. He was alone, and he began to sing them. There was no gathered audience, nor praise from passers by, but in an intentional display of what he thought was strength, he made sure those around him heard the anger and hate of a song that he heard as he strutted away.

Scripture came to my mind as I heard them, and it remains as true today as when it was written. "Their throats are open graves, their tongues practice deceit. The poison of vipers is on their lips. Their mouths are full of cursing and bitterness." (Romans 3:13-14 NIV)

I want my children to know that words are powerful. The foul mouths of those people weren't helping them draw closer to their friends in any meaningful way, but they were pulling them away from peace. They were creating a burden for themselves and will experience an increasing pressure to be bound to that behavior. For what? The superficial impression of their friends? An illusion of strength? It isn't worth it.

Healing, hope, and happiness never came though cursing.

- Using what God has given us to the best of our ability is no less than he expects. We're raised usually being taught to be self confident, and I don't think self confidence is wrong unless it is to the exclusion of God. It would be a foolish test to ask him to do for us something he's already made possible in us. Then there are those times things are beyond us. Beyond our abilities. Beyond our control. Don't push God away trying to handle those things yourself. Don't turn away in despair. Everything we have and everything we need is in him. "I can do all things through Christ which strengtheneth me." (Philippians 4:13 KJV)

- Old enough to drive, a hot summer afternoon found me with two other boys out in the middle of Black Lake in a twelve foot aluminum boat. The white perch and brim were going wild out in the cypress knees, and we were happy as a pup with two tails with every cork going out of sight. The weather seemed good when we'd started with just a few clouds, but little did we know that a front was moving into the area. All we were focused on was the fact that the fish were biting.

We saw the clouds coming in thicker, but the feeding frenzy continued. The thunder started rolling in the distance, and still we held on. Forget the ice chest! We were going to be like Peter when he pulled up the nets that were to the point of breaking, and fill the bottom of the boat. Finally, the wind picked up as the leading edge of the front started to roll over which apparently was the Lord's final way of telling us it was time to go home. Thankfully, it made the fish stop biting or I think it would have been too late.

The few boats that had remained out with us now flew by us and were gone before our boat could settle back down from their wake in the channel. One place you don't want to be in a lightning storm is in the middle of a lake in an aluminum boat. It's the equivalent of wrapping yourself in tinfoil and climbing to the top of a lone oak in the middle of a pasture under a thunderhead. It defies common sense. Making matters worse, Christopher Columbus had scratched his initials somewhere on the ancient boat motor we were now looking to for salvation. A few well placed lightning strikes nearby let us know we'd messed up and it was past time to get to the bank.

God knows a thing or two about fishing. I wonder how many Black Lake converts he got that day, as the lighting strikes seemed to encircle us on our way to the bank. I'm pretty sure the other boys in the boat renewed their faith that evening with the mosquito like hum of the small outboard motor rising up with our unspoken prayers. I know I was thinking about him. Wet and surprisingly cold, we made it back.

Shaken though we were, it would be a lesson well remembered. You can be distracted by blessings to the point that recognition of the one who gives them is lost. Lately, I hear the thunder and I feel the wind. I think it is time to get back home. Don't be caught in the middle of the lake because you're focused only on having a good time. Make sure you have peace in God.

Chapter IV

A Cardboard Fort

The rent house in Hodge we lived in had a combination bath and utility room. In that area we'd made the mistake of leaving a large container of baby powder within my firstborn's reach. A few unattended minutes was all it took for him to discover shaking the container made a big white cloud of fun. The washer, dryer, tub, shelves, walls–everything in a twenty foot radius had a coating of powder. On the floor in the middle of the mess, like a dumpling rolled out in flour, was our two year old son with a big ol' smile on his little ol' face.

I'd like to say that I embraced that moment as precious. I'd like to say it, but I'd be lying. It was a precious moment, but dad blew it. Instead of grabbing the camera and taking pictures in good humor, I couldn't see past the cleaning that had suddenly become necessary. Grumbling and growling, I worked to get it all back to normal.

My two year old's behavior could be excused, but mine really couldn't be. The problem was that I let selfishness obscure my view of the scene in front of me, instead of focusing on what was important.

"Let nothing be done through selfish ambition or conceit, but in lowliness of mind let each esteem others better than himself." (Philippians 2:3 NKJV) Putting others before ourselves doesn't always come naturally for human beings. We tend to consider only how we are personally affected by things, but it is when we put ourselves out of the way for the benefit of others that we are acting as children of God.

Being a dad has given me many, many, more opportunities to correct my focus. Some of those opportunities weren't nearly as cute. Like the time my offspring put an arrow in the hood of my truck or sailed the neighbor's mail down the creek. Come to think of it, my

A Cardboard Fort

focus on what's important should be razor sharp by now.

- Maw maw and paw paw Phillips were wonderful people. They'd gather all the grandchildren to stay over and play together. There was nothing quite like the thrill of the wind whipping around your head as you rode in the back of paw paw's old blue Ford. You could imagine you were flying as you stared up at the afternoon sky on the way to their house.

Paw paw loved to tease us by scratching us with his 5 o'clock shadow, then he'd settle into his football game. He got pretty vocal with it, but you'll have to forgive him. He enjoyed the Saints, and I'm just sorry he never got to see their Superbowl win.

Maw maw was always cooking up something in the kitchen, and it was always good. The smells alone that emanated from that stove and oven would make television chefs hang their heads in shame. I know she counted it as joy to see us going after her hot buttered cornbread and fresh purple hull peas like it was the best food on earth. And it was.

Chase, hide and seek, super heros, whatever the game might have been, we'd play outside until nearly dark, and when we came in there was always a warmth in that house. Not necessarily the temperature–genuine selfless love.

Mornings we would wake to the sound of old hymns coming from maw maw as she worked in the kitchen. I'm not saying I was crazy about waking up in those days anymore than you'd expect any other kid to be, but there was something, someone, in her that not everyone has. You could feel it. They knew what hard times were, and how far they'd come. When she said grace, you knew she meant it.

What I wouldn't give to be a little fella again and go into that kitchen and hug her! No words. She'd know how much I loved her by how tightly I'd squeeze her.

> "If I speak in the tongues of men or of angels, but do not have love, I am only a resounding gong or a clanging cymbal. If I have the gift of prophecy and can fathom all mysteries and all knowledge, and if I have a faith that can move mountains, but do not have love,

> I am nothing. If I give all I possess to the poor and give over my body to hardship that I may boast, but do not have love, I gain nothing."
> (1 Corinthians 13:1-3 NIV)

God is love, and we are commanded to love one another. Whatever our gifts, love will outlast them all. Never underestimate the value of a life lived in faith. Even the simplest of acts can have a tremendous impact in the lives of others when they are done out of love, and it is love which will be remembered when other memories fade. Maw maw was such a life.

The years quickly went by and those times passed in the wink of an eye. Maw maw and paw paw are both gone now, but not in my heart.

- Pilate had a sign fastened to the cross that read, "Jesus of Nazareth, The King of the Jews." The chief priests of the Jews protested, asking that the sign not say, "The King of the Jews," but only that Jesus claimed to be king and not that he was. Pilate spoke, "What I have written, I have written." He would not change it. (see John 19:19-22)

Perhaps Pilate was mocking the ones which had brought Jesus to him by what he had written, or perhaps he indeed felt something special about the one crucified. A sign might be rewritten, but doing so would not change the truth.

Today as then, the world wants to deny Jesus his rightful place. It approaches Pilate hoping to rewrite who Jesus was. Mocking him, it wants him to be nothing more than the third recorded criminal that died on that hill, but the truth still cannot be changed: Jesus is king!

I am grateful that on that day, despite everything happening to him, I was on his heart. Despite everything about me, he chose the cross so that I could have everlasting life.

Who is Jesus to you?

- Some time ago, my son and a neighborhood friend decided to build a fort out in the woods near our house. He was completely open to me about his endeavors, explaining that the cardboard they were using was trash that a contractor working on a nearby construction site was generating. They were obviously having a good time, the woods they were playing in

A Cardboard Fort

belonged to my family, and nothing seemed amiss. The answers I had seemed right, and I was filtering though my own experiences. What could possibly be wrong with young boys building a fort?

As it turned out, the "discarded" cardboard they'd discovered was actually a type of cardboard used to pour concrete. It wasn't from a waste bin–it was on a sort of storage trailer. Several afternoons of their labor that hadn't gone adequately supervised resulted in a fort at least four decimal places in value.

They weren't trying to hide anything. It was visible from the construction site, and they truly didn't think they were taking anything of worth. Not much later, I got word that the foreman had filed a police report about the apparent theft.

In that moment, I was faced with a choice: perhaps the contractor had insurance and we could lay low until trouble blew over, or we could confess and offer to try to make amends. Doing the right thing isn't always easy, but we don't do them because of how much it takes from us to do them–we should do them because they are right! My son was looking up to me at that same moment, and even had I avoided whatever monetary trouble that might have been on the horizon, I would not have avoided the voice of my conscience.

Son in tow, I came forward to talk to the people on the job site. Unfortunately, the workers on the site that day were mostly Hispanics that spoke poor English, so I knew that I'd have to return.

The thought of my teenage son being in serious trouble was pushing me into a place of helplessness. I prayed anyway. I knew I was making the right decision to come forward, but it had all the appeal of licking hornets. Salvaging what we could of the undamaged cardboard, we cleaned up the mess that evening, not quite sure what tomorrow held. Nothing like a little anticipation to make the moment sweeter.

The next day, I was able to speak to the man in charge. Apologetically as I was able, I blundered through an ineloquent confession of what the boys had done, and my son did too. He appreciated that I'd been honest and said that he believed they'd meant no harm. He turned out to be a biker that rode for a child advocacy group. What were the chances? There were no chances.

God knew the boys were going to make a mistake. He knew we were going to be honest. He knew we would need someone approachable that understood kids for the best possible outcome. In control all along, he was waiting for a greater realization in me that alone I am not enough to handle everything, but he was with me. Despite my own inabilities to see a way out, I sought him and he answered me in a way better than I'd hoped.

The gentleman spoke to the owner and no charges were pursued and the debt was forgiven. Had I gone the other way, I can't say exactly how it would have gone, but it wouldn't have been well. God wouldn't have been in it.

CHAPTER V

HAZMAT HONEYMOON

"When they saw the star, they were overjoyed." (Matthew 2:10 NIV)

Wise men from the east came to Jerusalem following a star, seeking Jesus. To me, there is wonderful mystery surrounding exactly who these men were. Neither Jewish nor citizens of the realm to which they'd traveled, but scholarly men that observed the heavens. Deemed worthy of an audience with king Herod, yet Herod was not the king they sought.

How they started their journey is not written, but there is no suggestion of an unholy origin of their knowledge. Whatever their backgrounds may have been, they'd learned something so important that they left the comfort of their own lands, traveled far, and boldly asked in the court of another, "Where is the one who has been born king of the Jews?" An assumption that the child king would be known and accepted shows the depth of the revelation that had been given to them.

Imagine Mary's amazement as these strangers presented gold, frankincense, and myrrh! Overjoyed, there was no idleness in these men. The fact they left with nothing material or political points to more than an idle encounter, and their departure was kept safe by God.

Have you seen the star?

Once more, events are heralding a special appearance. Open your heart through prayer to the same sweet Spirit the wise men sought. No costly gift is needed to present yourself, but you can receive a costly gift with only a contrite heart. His love for you is why he came, and he is coming again because of love for those who will be his.

Don't let commercialism dominate your holiday, and don't despair for bygone days.

Approach Christmas believing and experience it as a child again. His child.

- Shoes in the floor. Dishes all over the kitchen counter and in the sink. School papers and books on the dining table. Laundry on the couch. Soda cans, drink cups, plastic bottles in my son's room. Indescribable carnage in my daughter's room. I know I've got to begin the daily routine of helping to straighten, and I'm wondering where the matches are, but I restrain myself.

You see, the shoes came from my wife's feet that were tired from working. The dishes served the food that kept everyone fed. The papers and books are from two good kids that are growing up fast. The laundry means we all have clean clothes to wear, and who doesn't hate folding clothes? My son's room is a lot more organized than it used to be. My daughter's room, well, lucky for her she'll always be my little girl.

Putting the mess into perspective takes a lot of the edge off the violation of my sense of order. The kids will probably gripe, but they'll do their part. Call it an exercise in responsibility, because sometimes it takes more effort to get them to do something than to simply do it.

My point is, all the chaos doesn't fit my personality, but the family it belongs to does. Don't stress over the stuff that won't matter tomorrow, and if you have to wonder, then it likely needs to be reassessed before you go looking for matches.

Stones can make a house, but only people can make a home.

> "So we fix our eyes not on what is seen, but on what is unseen, since what is seen is temporary, but what is unseen is eternal." (2 Corinthians 4:18 NIV)

• Traveling to work has proven to be a good time for prayer. Being not long before dawn, there are few distractions and I'm alone. There have been mornings that I haven't, but I've been trying to pray no matter how I'm feeling.

"Jesus, be welcome with me," I began in the darkness.

As I prayed, I started examining my own heart. Like a light shining down the road casting long shadows from things beside it, the holiness of God made clear my shortcomings, each one with its own shadow of fear trying to twist in the light.

I remembered his word, "There is no fear in love, but perfect love casts out fear..."

Not that I hadn't confessed these things before that were bothering me, but again I found myself laying them at his feet. Compared to the holiness of God, a man's heart isn't much worth saving–and I was feeling it. Miserably.

"Lord have mercy on me," I prayed for the shameful things of my heart. Then I turned my attention from those feelings to the One to whom I was confessing. Was God angry with me for them?

I tried to imagine in that moment what God would say, and what I heard was this, "I know these things, and I still love you." Tears began to flow. I didn't push them away, I welcomed them like new hope.

Whatever God sees in me, I can't say. I'm thankful he reached out to me. He's reaching out to you too.

- "A merry heart does good, like medicine, but a broken spirit dries the bones." (Proverbs 17:22 NKJV)

Honeymoons are a special time of getting to know one another. When my wife and I married, we decided to spend time in Texas. From Arlington's Six Flags to the Fort Worth Zoo, there was an endless amount of things to do, and there was no one that I wanted to do them with more than her.

At times like that you've got to keep your strength up, so most mornings we'd eat breakfast. The first few days we loaded up at a breakfast buffet in anticipation of everything on the agenda. One item in particular seemed to be a favorite of my sweetie. Eggs. Not that she didn't try other things, but a good portion of her fare consisted of them.

Perhaps I should give a little history of our relationship here. I don't remember exactly at what point in it that I began to pass gas in front of her, but it was long before people would have been inclined to think of us as going steady. Otherwise, I probably would have had a gas bubble go to my brain and died long before we ever had the chance to say, "I do." Maybe it's a guy thing, but regardless of what I've eaten, or when I eat it, nature takes its course and necessitates the occasional prudent life saving release of pressure.

The love of my life is a different story. I'd convinced myself by this time that she simply didn't have the need to do the same. Apparently, her internal machinery lived up to an emissions standard that came out long after I'd left the assembly line. She was pretty, funny, and green friendly–what more could a man ask for?

An early start on the day at the hotel meant that much more time I'd get to spend with this amazing woman. I finished up a few minutes in the shower and stepped out of the bathroom to get dressed. The tiny currents made by opening the door immediately stirred an unholy presence in that hotel room. Confusion gripped my mind as I struggled between the desire to run and a sense of panic like a drowning man. "Oh my gosh! What is that smell?!" Moving across the room toward the door, I expected to be greeted outside by a Hazmat team in full gear ushering guests away because of some horrible chemical accident nearby.

Halfway across the room, I notice my wife face down in the pillows. Raising up she starts laughing, lifts a pillow, and starts fanning.

Over indulgence on our trip and all those heavy breakfasts had taken their toll. Embarrassed, she'd waited until I went into the bathroom to get ready before letting it go. Merciful heaven, did she ever let it go! Judging by the odor, it must have been incubating our entire relationship. The pillow she was using only stirred the acrid fumes, renewing the strength of it with each motion. Her laughter at my reaction completed my disillusionment: the angel I'd married was human after all.

I opened the hotel door hoping there wouldn't be an explosion of vapor like from a sauna that would draw the attention of security. Later she told me she felt so ashamed at that simple thing that she wanted to die, but through silliness and lots of fresh air, we drew a little closer that day. I wouldn't trade a minute of it, but I might have asked her to cut back on the eggs.

Chapter VI

GONE NOT FORGOTTEN

Just because someone isn't what you expect doesn't mean they aren't sincere toward the Lord. God isn't grading us on eccentrics. He is looking for hearts that are sincere toward him.

John the Baptist wore clothing made of camel hair, lived in the wilderness, and ate locust. No doubt, he raised a few eyebrows in his day. Yet Jesus said no man born among men was greater than him. Don't look down on others simply because they aren't like you in every way. There are no perfect people, but thankfully there are people changed by our perfect God–even when they aren't quite what others expect.

- We had a gas stove when I was a small boy. The matches for it were held by a ceramic chicken. Mama taking matches from its back to light the fire gave it purpose. It was a cute object that had probably been there as long as I could remember.

One day, mama and daddy got into an argument. Daddy lost his temper and being near the stove, grabbed the match holder then smashed it into a million pieces. Already confused by what was happening, when I saw the blameless little bird in pieces my heart broke with it.

I was too young to understand why they were fighting, but I understood the pieces scattered around were not going back together. I could not have known at the time that it was a portent of their relationship.

Their divorce some years later left me in pieces just like that match holder. Unlike human hands incapable of reassembling shattered porcelain, God was not done with me. What happened became part of who I am, but it did not define how he wanted things to be.

None of us pass through life without pain, but do you know that there is someone who offers beauty for ashes and joy for mourning? Are you holding back the pieces of something that's been shattered in your life? Are you holding back the pieces of you?

> "Though you have made me see troubles, many and bitter, you will restore my life again; from the depths of the earth you will again bring me up." (Psalm 71:20 NIV)

Through prayer, give Jesus the pain you're holding and ask him to restore your soul. He will if you will honestly seek him!

- God is worthy of all praise, but he is not vain in any human sense.

He does not care how many times you try to squeeze his name in through the course of a day, how many posts you share on your chosen social network threatening condemnation if you scroll by without clicking, nor how much you carry on about a preacher or a book. Souls are not won by showing other people how religious you can be. The praise he desires should be heartfelt and personal, never out of an obligatory sense that we need to prove to our fellow man how good we are.

Being Christian does set a person apart from the world. Salvation is the starting point, then a believer does enter into a sanctification process whereby Christ is shaping us into who he wants us to be. It is a process that won't end until we see Jesus. People can be recognized by their fruit, just as a tree can. However, if a well meaning believer can't have a conversation without talking about a television preacher, speaking the name of Jesus seven times, or declaring that no other understanding save their own could be good enough for God then they threaten to push away the very people with which they want to share the Gospel.

Live by the Word. Be led by the Spirit. Let people see the light in you, but don't shove your candle in their eye. Instead, pass the flame when they uncover theirs.

- Remember static? Before digital technology, you had to find radio stations manually. As you turned the tuner the sound would crackle and pop from every sort of unknown interference. Eventually the meaningless noise would give way as you approached that sweet spot where your station was located. Then your music would start playing. If you were really high tech, maybe you'd grab a blank cassette to record your favorite song and pray the DJ didn't talk over the beginning of it.

I don't know about the rest of you, but I have to deal with a lot of spiritual static. What do I mean by spiritual static? It can be too much emphasis on blessings without considering who is giving them, or too much focus on misfortune without considering who carries us. Perhaps nagging obligations generated in day to day living. Even in church, thoughts and feelings can crop up that seem so wrong. All are distractions from our human nature, and the Devil is there to amplify the interference.

God understands better than us the things we face. After all, he is God. He does not stop loving you as you are turning through all the static trying to find him. His frequency location will not change: Jesus.

I'm telling myself even as I am telling you– keep seeking. When we are best tuned in to him is where the static goes away.

"Ask and it will be given to you; seek and you will find; knock and the door will be opened to you. For everyone who asks receives; the one who seeks finds; and to the one who knocks, the door will be opened." (Matthew 7:7-8 NIV)

- We're all in the same boat. It's called humanity. We're all on the same sea. It's called life. We're all facing the same storm. It's called mortality.

Inevitably, the sea becomes unsettled by the wind. We reach a point where our humanity is challenged. Looking to those of us in the boat with you provides no calm, no answers.

Are you being tossed about by the waves? Afraid, confused, maybe even angry? Do you think there is something in you or about your life that God can't take?

Don't look to those in the boat with you for the answers. Even the best captains are eventually at the mercy of the sea. Instead, consider for a moment the One who approaches you walking on the water.

> "A strong wind was blowing and the waters grew rough. When they had rowed about three or four miles, they saw Jesus approaching the boat, walking on the water, and they were frightened. But

he said to them, 'It is I. Don't be afraid.' Then they were willing to take him into the boat, and immediately the boat reached the shore where they were heading." (John 6:18-21 NIV)

He walked on water then, and he can still walk on it! If you want to arrive safely on the shore, then it's time to take Jesus into the boat. With all my soul, I believe in him!
• A friend of mine shared the caution, "If you are too open minded, your brains will fall out."

What great advice! Being open to new ideas and listening to other points of view is an intelligent approach to life. That is, until someone tries to reason away divine sovereignty. Sin at the dawn of time is still sin. It is unaffected by societal changes in perception. Neither has any philosophy, religion, or rejection of the same altered our need for the redeeming sacrifice of Christ.

You can still love a person and not accept their sin. Whatever their arguments for their choices may be, only God's word on it matters.

Gone Not Forgotten

It does not make you unenlightened nor phobic to stand for what's right. What it does make you is faithful.

- While my child's piano lesson was taking place at Mount Olive church, I decided to visit an old cemetery nearby which had a Confederate grave.

Older cemeteries can be interesting and are a touch of history. Research into my family name has found me walking through quite a few of them. The markers that people used to honor the memory of their loved ones come in so many forms. Marble and granite are common for more recent graves, but iron ore and petrified wood can be seen marking graves all over north Louisiana. The fact is our modern traditions did not dictate how families marked them. Either the families could not afford the more expensive products of a stone-cutter, or they simply weren't available.

The passage of time takes it's toll on even the better made markers dating only two centuries ago. Sweet words engraved from the love of those who were left behind wear away. Stones long untended fall and themselves become buried. Only the surviving family of many of the unusual ones could have hoped to identify who lay beneath them, and they too are now gone.

As I walked among the stones, I wondered how many were resting that had no remaining marker or no descendents that knew who they were. Examining the ones not faring well, a sense of sorrow began to grow as I thought of those forgotten.

Crickets sang a slow and peaceful song somewhere in the distance, and a gentle breeze blew over me as if God were saying in response, "I have not forgotten them."

> "Do not be amazed at this, for a time is coming when all who are in their graves will hear his voice and come out. Those who have done what is good will rise to live, and those who have done what is evil will rise to be condemned." (John 5:28-29 NIV)

Not one soul who has passed before us is beyond his reach. If we do not hear the trumpet heralding the return of the Lord with our mortal ears, but live the span of our days still we need not fear the grave. Death has been defeated, and we will not be forgotten!

Chapter VII

MEETING AT THE STUMP

Science is real, but it is no substitute for divine providence. God created an ordered universe and blessed man with a capacity for understanding it, but a vision of God will never be discovered through radio telescope, neither will he be disproved beneath a microscope. Slamming subatomic particles together may reveal many things, but it will not reveal the heart of God.

If you want to know what God is like, it is only logical to start with his greatest revelation of himself, Jesus Christ. Great philosophers and brilliant minded men ponder much and may offer insight into the natural world, but the only revelation we will have of God is that which he offers us.

So if you're looking for answers to satisfy the soul within, seek its maker. Look to his Word, his Son, his Spirit and not men who would deny him.

Those content in their sins will scoff. The proud will substitute the need for God with something else. However, those open to him receive new life beyond the flesh!

"He who believes in me, as the Scripture has said, out of his heart will flow rivers of living water." (John 7:38 NKJV) Earthly water can only quench an earthly thirst, but living water satisfies the soul.

Lives become wastelands, but living water can restore even the most barren ground. I'm proof.

- When I pray healing for others, the image of the paralyzed man being lowered through the roof to Jesus comes into my mind.

"Since they could not get him to Jesus because of the crowd, they made an opening in the roof above Jesus by digging through it and then lowered the mat the man was lying on." (Mark 2:4 NIV) It's a powerful image to consider. The men moving in their faith, not knowing exactly what was about to happen, but trusting in the goodness of the Lord. They could have been discouraged by the crowd they knew they would have to struggle through to reach him, but they did not turn away. They could have given up when they saw how difficult it would be to present their friend, but they didn't.

Seeing their faith, he first met the man's greatest need. Forgiveness. Then proving his authority to give it, he healed the man who then took up his mat and walked out in full view of everyone.

Praying healing for others is a sign of our faith. The crowd is discouraging and there are obstacles in our way, but we don't have to tear a hole in any roofs to reach the Lord. We have only to be sincere in our desire to see him act in the lives of our friends. Take the time to present your friends to the Lord. It matters to God. Does it matter to you?

Prayer changes things, and prayer has changed me.

- As long as there is human nature, man will always contend with racism. However, in the light of recent news it is pleasantly ironic that in this Georgia metropolis, I saw people of many colors all walking together, eating together, and being nothing less than civil to one another.

The green people weren't smashing in storefronts because the blue people had someone in their group that they didn't approve. The blue people weren't looking down their noses as they passed the other on the street. Just everyone getting along. Imagine the disap pointment down the street at CNN.

Exceptions? There always will be. No doubt racism is here too, but it was refreshing that I didn't witness it knowing how the media is so quick to crucify the entire South for an incident singled out of a cornucopia of the evils of humanity.

Blue killing blue or green killing green doesn't create the same kind of media frenzy. How noble of them! The unwary can't see how they fan the flames of hatred in the name of "fair" journalism.

Here's a quote worthy of their air time, "ANYONE who claims to be in the light but hates a brother or sister is still in the darkness." (1 John 2:9 NIV) God made us all different for his good reasons, none of which included the measure of a man's worth by the color of his skin.

Hang in there CNN. Maybe you'll have a fresh riot tomorrow.

- "Let the morning bring me word of your unfailing love, for I have put my trust in you. Show me the way I should go, for to you I entrust my life." (Psalm 143:8 NIV)

On the road and traveling far from home, I watched crimson and purple chase away the last of the night. Gazing toward heaven, it felt as though the sky might burst as unseen angels transformed the horizon into a tapestry of gold.

You can think of the sunrise as an impressive visual display of physics with an attitude that it's just another day dawning, or you can think of it as another day closer to the coming of the Lord.

Be warned. It's not just the next day in an endless number of tomorrows. As sure as the sun will also set, the world as we have known it is drawing to a close. Scripture tells us when we see all the things happening now, look up!

Perhaps generations will pass, but it may be in your lifetime that Jesus will return for those who are his. Are you entrusting your life to him, or is God something impersonal you adorn your life with to create an illusion of everything being okay?

Invite him into your heart and the sunrise won't be the same!

- Daddy loved to fish. This particular afternoon found me with him at one of the ponds close to our camp house out in the Walker community just off the Transport Cemetery Road. I was at an age where playing on the sandy bank with a stick was every bit as entertaining as fishing.

Making a little too much noise resulted in a plea to be quiet, but he still kept fishing. I went on playing. The nearby minnows would dart in the shallows right along with dad's patience when I would stamp my feet. He asked me to stop, and he kept on fishing.

Maybe I took it as a challenge. I'm not sure now what was going through my head, but in a glaring display of the restlessness of a child, I had to slap my foot on that bank one more time. As he started toward me I knew I'd gone too far.

I'd made a number of mistakes that afternoon, what was one more? I ran. Up the hill and away from certain doom I went. Not even halfway up the hill, terror took over when I realized he was right behind me. Like a scene from an educational program where a lion is chasing a baby deer, you knew it was not going to end well, and the narrator was going to be talking about how it was nature's way. Man, did I feel sorry for that deer.

I didn't know where I was running. Logic in me had been abandoned the moment daddy threw down his fishing pole. Through one of the gardens by the camp and into the woods I went. It was no good. Dad was right there–I gave up.

We had a meeting at a nearby stump where he could sit, and he showed me the error of my ways. I didn't get many spankings from daddy, and I don't remember any that I didn't deserve. It was discipline, not abuse. The behind receiving correction was the same one he lovingly removed a treble hook on which I sat down on another occasion. Also, in his

Meeting at the Stump

defense, I can assure you the treble hook incident hurt far worse and the pain lasted far longer than the punishment given me there in those woods. He was upset, but he never stopped loving me.

> "Endure hardship as discipline; God is treating you as his children. For what children are not disciplined by their father? If you are not disciplined–and everyone undergoes discipline–then you are not legitimate, not true sons and daughters at all. Moreover, we have all had human fathers who disciplined us and we respected them for it. How much more should we submit to the Father of spirits and live! They disciplined us for a little while as they thought best; but God disciplines us for our good, in order that we may share in his holiness. No discipline seems pleasant at the time, but painful. Later on, however, it produces a harvest of

righteousness and peace for those who have been trained by it." (Hebrews 12:7-11 NIV)

Chapter VIII

LIFTOFF

The new year makes us stop to consider time. Days gone by and days to come, "He has made everything beautiful in its time. He has also set eternity in the human heart, yet no one can fathom what God has done from beginning to end." (Ecclesiastes 3:11 NIV)

We all experience good and bad through the course of time. Some things in time we welcome, and some we don't. Never the less, time has a certain mastery over our mortal existence, and there is an order to things created over which we have no control.

Although there is so much to enjoy in this life, its satisfactions are only temporary. The longing for knowing you're rooted in something more lasting–that desire is of God. Until that desire is satisfied, you will never truly be satisfied. You will always be focused on the next earthly pleasure, and, as wonderful as it may be, it will not last.

No one can fully wrap their minds around God, but God asks to embrace the soul of man. This is the answer to what makes us complete, "I know that everything God does will endure forever. Nothing can be added to it and nothing taken from it. God does it so that people will fear him." (Ecclesiastes 3:14 NIV) Do you reverence him with your life?

Where we find ourselves in time does not determine the dispensation of his love. His love is our great equalizer and from the highest to the lowest among us he wants us know it.

I hope your new year is bright in that knowledge with blessing upon blessing.

- I am careful with the family finances, and I don't go nuts with the plastic, but after last year I was feeling the squeeze. Different things that I simply could not pay for outright kept mounting up against my wallet that went on credit.

Making payments on that credit card bill was possible even before filing our taxes, but still I was letting it worry me too much. It seemed like such a large amount. However, I'd failed to consider a key item that was different on our return this year. Expecting much less on our refund, we received more.

God wants us to use good sense and not get ourselves into preventable binds, but he also wants us to trust that he's going to take care of us when we can't see the way. "Cast all your anxiety on him because he cares for you." (1 Peter 5:7 NIV)

In the end I received one dollar more on my federal income tax refund than I owed. Coincidence? Every good thing is at the orchestration of God. We should expect more, financial or otherwise, and receive in abundance. Starting with me.

- Lazarus, friend of Jesus, had been dead for four days. Deeply moved by his death, he went to the tomb. After the entrance stone had been removed, he thanked the Father for his faithfulness. "When he had said this, Jesus called in a loud voice, 'Lazarus, come out!'" (John 11:43 NIV)

His friend was dead no longer, but still wore the trappings of the grave when he came out. Life had been restored to him, but it was only by removing the grave clothes that he was able to move more freely.

Raising people from the dead was not a miracle reserved only for the time Jesus walked the earth. I know, because outside the darkness of the grave formed by sin, Jesus called me from spiritual death which is as real as death of the body.

Like the grave clothes of Lazarus, there have been things restricting my ability to move and see clearly, but I'm not the man that I was before I came from that tomb. Pride, doubt, and fear are bindings from which I'm breaking free, but, thank God, he has called my name!

"But as many as received Him, to them He gave the right to become children of God, to those who believe in His name." (John 1:12 NKJV) With the same love he had for his friend Lazarus, he is calling you to new and everlasting life. Come out of the grave!

- Monday, my better half sent a text message to tell me good morning. Imagine a little boy getting passed a note in grade school from his crush. It's the same thing. I was glad for the distraction because I was in a dreary work day mode. Enduring the onslaught of being my own worst enemy with the added pressure of work.

I don't know everything that was going on in her mind–texting has its limitations, but we were on the same wavelength. Her message said, "I wish we didn't have to work–that we were sitting on a pier fishing in the mountains. Away from all the bad in the world."

Mountain piers are in short supply, but there was a welcome warmth in the idea. Lord help us, there is so much bad in the world. People that want to kill us for having faith in a loving God, living under a government that seems to embrace every god but ours, and everything is poised on the edge of destruction.

Before I lose you, I'm not a doom and gloomer. We're not meant to go around everyday as if we were waiting on a funeral, but for believers I think a celebration will soon begin.

Maybe the thought of "the end" puts fear in your heart, or maybe the thought of judgment makes you feel ashamed. Ask God to take that fear and shame from you and to give you a greater revelation of his love. The end is also a beginning.

I wish when I was young that Revelations had been better explained to me. There are frightening things in it, but for believers it was meant as encouragement as well as warning. We will face trouble and things will get worse, but keep your faith because when we're living in the time as we are now—Jesus is about to return!

On the other hand, if you're unwilling to accept Jesus as Lord and Savior because you're satisfied in the life you think you have without him, then it is right to fear. Seek him and ask for forgiveness and help while you are able.

I want to be ready. I want you to be ready. Make sure you know where you stand.

I know that eye has not seen nor ear heard the things that God has prepared for those that are his. I'm sure heaven is unimaginably greater than earthly comparisons, but I sent a text back to Tonia, "In heaven. Three friends with cane poles. Me, you, and Jesus." The thought felt right in my soul. We are in the homestretch.

- "The fear of the Lord is the beginning of knowledge, but fools despise wisdom and discipline." (Proverbs 1:7 NIV)

Liftoff

Science always fascinated me in high school. Many times I remember mixing together things in the laboratory classroom that would have made a seasoned chemist cringe. Even after school, I continued to dabble in experiments just for fun. Take rocketry, for example.

Model rockets naturally caught my interest as a youth, and I revisited the hobby not long after my wife and I were married. Not content with the small commercially available solid rocket motors, I took it upon myself to explore a bit of do-it-yourself.

Carefully, I followed instructions produced by other amateur rocketeers and eventually produced a suitable propellant to make much larger rockets. Satisfied that my design was correct, I constructed a model containing the untested engine. Giddy with excitement, I wanted to show off the launch to my better half.

I used an electrical launch system, so in case there was a problem we would not be close to it. I thought we were at a safe distance from the experiment.

Three, two, one. Liftoff! For a moment there was a gratifying roar as the rocket seemed to be about to take to the sky. However, only a few feet from the launch pad it stalled and turned at a frightening angle far too horizontal to the ground. And pointing at my wife.

I'm not sure if she was moving for cover before or after it turned her way, but I learned she is way quicker than I'd ever given her credit. It became a surreal slow motion scene that was a little fuzzy, but what I am sure of was that it exploded before it traveled any further. A sound like a thunderclap punctuated my underestimation of the need for precautions.

No more rocket was a good thing. Well, almost. You see, the explosion caused the nose cone I'd used to become a projectile. Despite its light weight the force was sufficient to place a dent in the trunk of my folks car that happened to be parked nearby. Didn't see that one coming. As the smoke and debris settled, I was grateful to find that we were intact if a little rattled.

I continued to enjoy the hobby for a while afterwards, but for some reason my wife never caught my enthusiasm. Go figure.

Chapter IX

WHAT COULD POSSIBLY GO WRONG

Commencement for vacation Bible school was a microcosm of human behavior. The little ones on the platform seemed to exhibit the full spectrum of Christian faith.

While the leaders sang and made motions for the songs, a few of the youngest children were jubilant and unhindered by pride. Others were probably eager to please mom and dad. Of course, some rolled around on the floor not responding or looked more to their peers than the front.

Then one particular sweet little girl stood there with fear in her eyes. She was paying careful attention to how she was being led and doing her best, but she wasn't smiling.

Had she fully realized how much everyone watching was prepared to forgive any mistakes and wanted her to be happy, surely it would it have made a difference.

Maybe I'm the only one that felt a sting of guilt of not being a reflection of the happiest of those littlest ones. Perhaps I've spent far too much of my life rolling around on the floor. How many of us could stand with that little girl, perhaps trying our best, but in need of surrendering our fears? I know God wants us to be happy and secure in his love.

"Peace I leave with you; my peace I give you. I do not give to you as the world gives. Do not let your hearts be troubled and do not be afraid." (John 14:27 NIV) Lord, help me to trust as I should. A child of God does not have to be afraid!

- Mosaics can be made from broken objects. Without the artisan's hand the bits and pieces are without value, but inlaid with his skill they become something greater, something beautiful. At times the material may be broken further with each tiny piece being made to fit into the purpose envisioned for it. We are God's mosaic.

By trusting in him, we are being fashioned into something greater, something beautiful. New believer or old, we are sometimes broken before him as we struggle with our human nature. We may feel our lives are fragmented and our hearts shattered.

Although all we see are pieces, God sees a masterpiece. The enemy will always say there is no reason to continue, no reason to keep fighting, "But you, Lord, are a shield around me, my glory, the One who lifts my head high." (Psalm 3:3 NIV)

- Satan is not my favorite subject, but he is real. He attacks us through our mortality, and people become conditioned by his influence to question the love of God at the first sign of discomfort. He's efficient at what he does, ruthless, and relentless. The one who introduced humankind to sin desires that you would die unrepentant and without hope. It is his way of lashing out at the God who created him. "The thief does not come except to steal, and to kill, and to destroy. I have come that they may have life, and that they may have it more abundantly." (John 10:10 NKJV)

Satan is bent on taking the life of faith Jesus desires for you. When troubles come, and they come to us all, will you listen to the obnoxious and boisterous voice of the world, "There is no God," or will you listen to the voice of truth, "For the Lord is good and his love endures forever; his faithfulness continues through all generations." (Psalm 100:5 NIV) A God that loves you, or a Devil that hates you–to which voice are you responding?

Jesus made the restoration of the relationship God intended with himself possible through the cross. The Lord wants you to not simply exist, but to truly live! How do you begin? Call on Jesus, "For whosoever shall call upon the name of the Lord shall be saved." (Romans 10:13 KJV)

- I counted ten bars of soap and five bottles of body wash around the tub, and three bars of soap and one bottle of hand wash at the bathroom sink. Is there a soapaholics anonymous? I value personal hygiene, but this may be out of control at my home.

It actually brought to mind a scripture, "What sorrow awaits you teachers of religious law and you Pharisees. Hypocrites! For you are so careful to clean the outside of the cup and the dish, but inside you are filthy — full of greed and self-indulgence! You blind Pharisee! First wash the inside of the cup and the dish, and then the outside will become clean, too." (Matthew 23:25-26 NLT)

Wash the inside of the cup. A cup that is clean on the outside, but dirty on the inside can't serve its purpose. We can scrub with all the soap we want, get all perfumed up, and go to church, but until we have been cleaned on the inside we can't serve our purpose. No one wants to drink from a nasty cup.

Heavenly father, clean our cups completely that the water you offer us is not wasted. Let your spirit wash over our lives. Jesus, amen.

- "The greatest among you will be your servant. For those who exalt themselves will be humbled, and those who humble themselves will be exalted. Woe to you, teachers of the law and Pharisees, you hypocrites! You shut the door of the kingdom of heaven in people's faces. You yourselves do not enter, nor will you let those enter who are trying to." (Matthew 23:11-13 NIV)

As you read that, if your first concern was the fact that I used the New International Version of the Bible instead of the King James Version, then you may be one of the ones on my heart. I read this scripture across three different translations and I believe the essence of this scripture was preserved here. I thank God for the King James Version of the Bible. It is beautiful and has a poetic quality to its manner of speaking. It also can be very difficult to understand–not because of a lack of spiritual revelation, but because people today simply don't talk that way.

There are dangerous and erroneous translations out there, and if you have any doubt about one then ask your pastor. For example, there is no acceptable translation that eliminates the sin of homosexuality. If you see differences between one your brother is using and your favored version, then certainly point them out if it serves God. However, remember that even the King James Version is itself a translation of original Greek and Hebrew texts.

Don't overreact because your brother chooses a newer translation. That's kind of like getting upset because the Bible has been translated into Spanish.

This brings me to the second part of what's bothering me: the holier than thou folks. As I read that scripture I could not help but feel that people who wanted to be highly respected by men for how religious they seemed got on the Lord's nerves too. I don't always take my shoes off around people when I've been sweating, because I know my feet are going to stink. Some people like to wave them around under your nose oblivious that except for the grace of God, they are no different from anyone else.

They speak of humility, but they don't practice it. They shutter the light with themselves, and the lost wander right on by them because they're too busy arguing doctrinal differences, interpretations, and how no view other than their own could be valid.

I don't want to deliver a seeker friendly gospel that distorts the truth, and I don't want anything of me to get in the way of someone else really receiving it. Don't let anyone turn you from the true love of our savior, Jesus.

- A pleasant summer afternoon found me where my family had a couple of ponds and were living at the time. I was a boy, probably not much more than eleven. At that age I wasn't scared of much except wasps, snakes, and drowning.

Billy, my brother's friend, came over and asked to go fishing and he was welcome. He invited me to go along and I decided that I would. I mean, what could possibly go wrong on a backwoods pond except wasps, snakes, and drowning?

Only a little later, we found ourselves in an old boat with our Zebco rods in hand out in the biggest of the two ponds. If there is one thing I'd mastered at that age it was how to catch trees. It wasn't long before I'd hooked a big one. Try as I might the lure I was using wouldn't break free from the rotten spire standing in the water.

I guess Billy felt sorry for me and hated to be in on losing any of my dad's tackle. He made his way to it so it could be freed. The boat bumped the old tree causing the top of the stump to break off and fall into the bottom of the boat–right along with a wasp nest.

The resulting cloud of the little devils led me to a split second decision. I could stay in the boat and be stung ten times for every rock a kid ever threw at a nest, or I could jump into a snake infested pond and possibly drown. Did I mention that I could barely swim?

I don't think there was a right choice to be made, but I would have brought home the gold in dog paddling that afternoon. Swimming seemed to hide me from the swarming wrath as I made it to yet another stump. Looking back, there was poor Billy tangled up in lines and swatting.

An eternity seemed to pass but somehow we survived. He was eventually able to help me back into the boat. Billy had been stung seventeen times, but he'd be alright. I'd been spared even a single sting. The moral of the story depends on your point of view. For Billy it was, "Know when to cut the line." Mine may have been, "He who hesitates is lost."

Chapter X

Flaming Ice Picks

Sinners and even believers need repentance, but they also need direction and assurance about whom to seek and why. Don't just hit them over the head with the bible and say they are going to hell. Don't invalidate a person's desire to have more of God in their lives because they haven't received something you hoped for them. Instead, live a life that shows people the goodness of God. Speak of his holiness and what that means to you. Any gift you've been given–use it for his glory and not a measuring stick for the faith of others.

I was raised one denomination, but now attend another. There are good things about both, but I'm not convinced that any denomination has everything completely right. What I am convinced that I have right is Jesus! With all of my heart, I believe he was the embodiment of God on the earth. Redemption for us was his purpose here, and he accomplished it at the cross. I need him more than my next breath.

Are we focusing on him and asking for a deeper personal revelation, or just trying to act out the expectations of others so that we can be thought of as good? In the end, all that will matter is whether or not we truly loved him.

There is a lot that I don't like about myself. Inadequacies that I feel. Maybe just like you. As I sat outside this afternoon, I prayed. The blood shed at the cross still cleanses, still makes it possible for us to be changed, and still gives me hope.

I want it to give you hope too.

- If we had to depend on our feelings for assurance of salvation, no man's faith would survive. In the realm of our human experience, we share doubt, fear, and confusion. Working your way through those things alone brings despair, but submitting them to God in humble confession will surely bring change.

God wants the opportunity to reveal his love, so don't give up even when it may feel like your prayers aren't making it to the ceiling, much less heaven. He hears, he cares, he acts. Jesus lives, and he lives through our lives when we welcome him.

Deeper than my own heart, I believe the Spirit draws us even when our emotions seem hopelessly out of line. "...and I will ask the Father, and he will give you another advocate to help you and be with you forever, the Spirit of truth." (partial John 14:16-17 NIV)

- Go with the flow. We've all heard that expression. Whether you're talking about a river or life, if you go with the way currents naturally carry, you don't have to struggle so much. The world without God is moving away from him at an ever increasing pace, and we live in the world.

Turning to God goes against the flow around us, but the alternative is destruction. "For our struggle is not against flesh and blood, but against the rulers, against the authorities, against the powers of this dark world and against the spiritual forces of evil in the heavenly realms." (Eph 6:12 NIV)

Jesus loves us, and his grace will be sufficient for whatever we face so long as we are seeking him. Don't go with the flow!

- More than one gospel records the woman who'd been sick for many years that sought healing in Jesus. She thought, "If I just touch his clothes, I will be healed." A crowd moved with Jesus as he traveled to the house of Jairus to tend to his daughter. No doubt many reached out to touch him having heard of his miracles, each with their own reasons, some perhaps only to be able to say they'd touched the man about whom everyone was talking. The sick woman pressed in seeing her opportunity, and she touched him.

The connection her touch made was different. Desperate. She moved in the faith she had and reached out to God, and God reached back. As the tips of her fingers touched his garment, she was healed.

Jesus knew right away who it was, but in his humanity, he was unable to see her. He asked, "Who touched my clothes?" This wasn't spoken in an accusing tone, but he wanted her to know something. She knew she'd been healed and was afraid she'd somehow been overly bold. Although she trembled with fear before him, Jesus only encouraged her saying, "Take heart, daughter, your faith has healed you."

We are not unlike the woman that touched the hem of his garment with the things on our hearts. We make our way through the crowd, not necessarily knowing why the others are gathered around, who is genuine and who isn't. We just need to be desperate for a touch and move in the faith we have. He wants us to know peace and be healed.

Reach for the hem of his garment by going to your knees in prayer, then may God's love lift you up again. (Mark 5:25-34, Matthew 9:20-22, Luke 8:43-48)

- After arriving in the ER, I sat patiently with my mother in the waiting area. We were told by the admit clerk when my step dad was settled in a room from the transfer we would be asked to come. A crazy amount of time passed, and no one came. I went to the clerk, and they acted like they hadn't realized we were there and asked for insurance information. Then we were told to go to a side door and ring a bell to get inside. We did. We waited. People went back and forth in front of the opaque glass. No one let us inside. We rang again. We waited.

After ten minutes I went back to the admission window. They acted surprised and told me others had to let us in where we had been–they did not offer to help. I went back to the door pretty irritated at that point. I pressed the bell about twenty times in rapid succession. Lo and behold the electronic release on the door was opened. Going inside the man at the door was scowling, and he said, "You only have to ring once."

I was torn between laughing at him and punching him in the face, but I let it go. However, it made it clear that sometimes you need to be persistent to get results. "And will not God bring about justice for his chosen ones, who cry out to him day and night? Will he keep putting them off? I tell you, he will see that they get justice, and quickly. However, when the Son of Man comes, will he find faith on the earth?" (Luke 18:7-8 NIV)

• One morning when my daughter was three years old, she was coming to me down the hallway to the bedroom. Her smile was impossible to resist and naturally I wanted to squeeze all the sweetness out of her that I could get, so I bent down to pick her up. Instead of finding the embrace of my little girl, however, I just kept going to the floor.

A pain like a flaming ice pick being stabbed into my lower spine gripped me that I'd never experienced. Hitting my hands and knees, waves of pain rippled through my mind threatening to stop all conscious thought. I could not move, could not breathe, without making it worse. My wife was asking me what was wrong, and it was all I could do between held breaths to tell her that something was wrong with my back.

I managed to crawl to the living room not knowing what to do and not understanding what was happening. I didn't want to overreact which looking back was incredibly laughable. I was almost completely immobilized with blinding pain, yet I didn't want to call an ambulance.

My wife was about to call for help when I made up my mind to let her take me to the doctor's office. Slowly, very slowly, I literally crawled out of our house to the car. Every bump on the way was an explosion of agony that made hitting my thumb with a hammer seem like a good time. The nurse managed to help me into a wheelchair, and there I was finally able to get some relief.

It turned out that I'd developed a diffuse protrusion of a disc along my spine. My spinal cord was being impinged by entering a space that shouldn't have existed. Medicines have helped flare ups of the pain, but life hasn't been quite the same. I wasn't able to play with the kids the way I wanted. I can't explore places with my wife uninterrupted the way that I would like. If I've been on my feet for very long I'll begin to slap one foot on the ground as it becomes numb and at the same time the ice pick returns.

I would love for it to be taken from me, and while things have gotten better, it is a condition that hasn't gone away. Still I say, "Blessed be the name of the Lord from this time forth and for evermore." (Psalm 113:2 KJV)

If I questioned God's sovereignty over it, then it would pull me down. Nothing would be served by being bitter. I've wondered why it happened, but being inquisitive isn't a sin. I let it go on faith that it is not without good reason that it is something meant for me to endure. Our vision for the future can become impaired by suffering, but to give ourselves hope we must remind ourselves that this side of life is not even a moment in eternity.

Don't let a lack of understanding about your circumstances keep you from seeking the goodness of God!

CHAPTER XI

DUMPSTER DOG

Don't try to be a better person to redeem yourself. Be a better person because you have been redeemed. It isn't what we can do that will get us to heaven, but what has already been done.

One of the first scriptures many believers learn is John 3:16, "For God so loved the world, that he gave his only begotten Son, that whosoever believeth in him should not perish, but have everlasting life." (KJV) God held nothing back from us, not even his son, that we might be with him forever. Now, there is a God worthy of entrusting your life!

When we commit ourselves to the Lord, it is his giving spirit that has done everything necessary so that we can be counted as spotless before him. It is our appreciation for that, our response of love in return, that should shape our actions.

Believers are still flawed, still fallible, still human, but we have a reason to keep trying to make God smile: for God so loved us!

- "May my prayer be set before you like incense; may the lifting up of my hands be like the evening sacrifice." (Psalm 141:2 NIV) Why do believers raise their hands?

For me, there are many reasons. Sometimes it's an offering of thanks, sometimes it's in the hope of receiving something, and sometimes it's acknowledging my need for him to reach for me. I'm not waving my hands to empty air–I have a Savior watching over me. Like baptism, it is an outward sign of inward change, and biblically we have the liberty to do so.

Does God require it? No, but if it helps you express yourself, then lay down your pride and do it! Contrary to feelings fostered in some denominations, you will not burst into flames. I'm not criticizing believers that don't–I used to be one. I'm saying letting people see your faith even in small ways is a good thing. I think back to when my children were very young and reached up to me with tiny hands. Their expectation to be lifted up was impossible to ignore. Our heavenly Father is there for us in that way too–ready to lift us.

Will you lift up your hands?

- If a person's mind was represented by a cup, then certainly some people's cups would hold more than others, but they would all be limited. By comparison you might think of the mind of God as an ocean, endlessly extending beyond the horizon that our eyes can see. We can fill our cups from his ocean and know we have the water of life in them, but we cannot understand everything about God anymore than a cup can contain the ocean.

"Who can fathom the Spirit of the Lord, or instruct the Lord as his counselor? Whom did the Lord consult to enlighten him, and who taught him the right way? Who was it that taught him knowledge, or showed him the path of understanding?" (Isaiah 40:13-14 NIV) A person can stand on the shore with an empty cup denying the ocean before them that is getting their feet wet, or they can kneel down and fill their cup.

- If people denied you because they'd never met you, would it change the reality that you are who you are? If your trustworthy friends, with nothing to gain personally, told others about you and they still wouldn't believe, would it somehow invalidate your existence? Neither would it God. God said to Moses, "I am who I am." (partial Exodus 3:14 NKJV)

Jesus wants to meet you, and you don't have to clean up to do it–or figure out everything. Quite frankly, you can't. Ask him to be your savior, and he'll be right where you are. Lay your guilt, doubt, and fear before him and be changed with his help. A life of sin can be traded for an eternal life in God's favor, and the good news is that he loves you so much that he's already paid the price. Just choose to believe!

- There's a lady at my church that let's me know she is praying for me. When she tells me she is praying for me and looks into my eyes, I know that she is.

I don't think she would go looking for a storm, but if she was caught in one, I believe she would pray in the face of it. I know for a fact that there are some that would ridicule her for her faith, but God is moved by the prayers of his children.

I would rather she pray for me than ten thousand people would only flippantly say, "I'll be praying for you," in an effort to be polite who then never humble themselves. Where is the hope in people that claim to be Christian that make no room for divine intervention?

I'm not saying we do not have be realistic or that we are free to abandon common sense. When need arises, we should take advantage of ordinary things that can help us and apply the knowledge God has given us in the capacities we each have–then thank Him for them.

However, being a believer is not a fatalistic journey confined by the natural world. God is absolutely good and He is all powerful. We don't have to understand it, but we have to acknowledge and accept His holiness and omnipotence, or else our claims of faith have no lasting meaning.

Increase my faith, Lord, "Teach me to do your will, for you are my God; may your good Spirit lead me on level ground." (Psalm 143:10 NIV)

- My parents were both school teachers. They instilled a wonderful desire for learning in me. Some lessons were harder and have taken longer to learn than anything I ever did in a classroom, but I am thankful for the grace of the Lord in them–my parents and the lessons. Without a doubt, I'm still learning. At some point along the way they may have asked me not to follow them in public teaching, but I'm sure they wouldn't mind me sharing something of the hope that is in me.

Growing up in the flatlands of northern Louisiana back in the 80s was predictable. For example, if born a child of someone in the timber industry, the likelihood of escaping a similar fate dissipated with each campfire that they found themselves around with friends on a Friday night. It wasn't that the opportunity or ability to change wasn't possible. It was just unnecessary. Good friends, a good job, and strong family values meant a person could be content exactly where he found himself.

We had so many advantages here in that day that had nothing to do with economics. Belief in God was like chlorine in the water supply, and folks adhered to, "Start children off on the way they should go, and even when they are old they will not turn from it." (Proverbs 22:6 NIV) A few fought taking their parent's medicine and went on to get sick from the world, but you didn't get out without a dose of Jesus. So you weren't rich or famous. So what? You could be happy, because you were raised knowing what real fulfillment was.

I'm thankful my faith was born of that time and place, and I want to reach out with the desire to let others know, "...it shall come to pass, that whosoever shall call on the name of the Lord shall be saved." (partial Acts 2:21 NIV)

• The wedding is about to begin. People are still being gathered, and they are coming from where ever they may be found. We share in an invitation to a celebration that we do not deserve. Remember we did not furnish ourselves with the wedding clothes. Are we behaving as grateful guests of the King, or do we walk about in self admiration, forgetting what his garment of righteousness has covered? (see Matthew 22:1-14)

Lord, let my faith draw others, that they might come to know you as their loving Heavenly Father. Keep me mindful that it is through the love you proved at the cross that I am redeemed, not by how I was, how I am, or how I hope to become.

- One day, we acquired a silly, ignorant, soulful eyed puppy. As usual, we'd forgotten to get the garbage to the curb, so we had to make a trip to the dumpster. Someone had thrown out this puppy that looked like a cute stuffed animal lying there on the ground. Normally, I'd have tried to go my own way and not pay attention. That day was different. That day, I had my son with me.

My son inspected the little thing, and it raised up its head. Lying there in the filth, it recognized the voice of compassion as he spoke to it. It had the beginnings of mange, but you could tell that it was going to be an attractive dog. Maybe someone would throw it garbage food. Maybe someone would take it care of it. Maybe it would be okay. The truth was, it didn't have a chance.

So leaving the dump, I brought back a box to carry it so it wouldn't get nasty stuff and parasites everywhere, and we brought it home. We cleaned her up, took her to the vet, and have been taking care of her for a couple of weeks. My daughter wanted to call her Chloe, but I've been calling her "D D" which is short for dumpster dog. Dee Dee is loving, sweet, and playful. Just what a puppy was meant to be, but only because she was given compassion.

Wouldn't we only be dumpster dogs if God had passed us by? Instead, he helps us become the person he knows we can be. Having been shown this compassion, should we not share the hope that is in us? "Be kind and compassionate to one another, forgiving each other, just as in Christ, God forgave you." (Ephesians 4:32 NIV)

It's one thing to feel sorry for someone, and something else to act on it. One is not as good as the other. I want to make a difference. Lord, give me strength and wisdom to act more and more in compassion.

Chapter XII

Dating Anxiety

While my dad talked about trout fishing and Arkansas waterways with another man, I was happy to be the epitome of a nine year old boy. A container of worms gave me the opportunity to tease the man's daughter of the same age with big red wigglers.

Dangling one in front of her face was sure to be great sport. I thought no little girl was tough enough to handle bait. Instead of reacting in the terror I'd hoped, she slapped my arm away slinging the dirty worm right into my mouth. The chase was on around our daddy's legs, and she became a friend!

The way we meet people can appear so random on the surface.

Place a bunch of marbles in a jug and shake it and they will bump in to one another. Similarly, put a bunch of people on a planet and spin it and sooner or later some will meet. It's simply statistics, right? Well, not quite.

The laws of probability may demonstrate the likelihood of encounters between objects mathematically, but they aren't much use in explaining the different connections to all the people in our lives.

Whatever kinsfolk, neighbors, strangers, or friends are intersecting your life is not without the forethought of God. He saw all those people and knew you could overcome the bad, be a blessing to the good, and be a light to those living in darkness.

With his help you can do all those things. There is no one better suited for what he has for you to do among whom you are connected.

We are meant to be who we are, where we are, and when we are with divine reason. The life you have been given is not a random marble careening around in a jug.

Your connection with others, however small, is no accident. Ask God for the wisdom and strength to make the very best of every one of them.

> "We are therefore Christ's ambassadors, as though God were making his appeal through us. We implore you on Christ's behalf: Be reconciled to God." (2 Corinthians 5:20 NIV)

- My first real job was working as an assistant in the mainframe laboratory in college. It helped me get through some of my computer programming classes, and my inner nerd reveled in the greenish glow of the ancient IBM terminals. Long before energy compliance guidelines, you could warm your leftover burrito from the radiation emanating out of those screens. There was something magical about the roar of the gigantic dot matrix printer that I was sure was a wood chipper in another life spewing out my fellow students' work.

In the days before instant messaging, talking over a networked computer was like magic. You'd think, "There's someone logged on that I know. I'll message them 'Hello,'" or

"Look, there's that jerk that was bugging me about getting his report from the centralized printer. Oops! Too bad dude. I accidentally disconnected you." When you were logged on as a lab assistant the temptation was there to go mad with power.

There was just so much you could do with computers even in their infancy, and programming logic appealed to me. It was what I wanted to do. Despite doing well in all my classes I let one professor scare me away from the curriculum. Even though I'd been taught by the department head in the prerequisite classes, she walked in and announced everything that I should already know about computers coming into her class and I knew none of it. Fear drove me away from the curriculum.

The abrupt change in plans left me in between majors without my sweet lab job so I soon found myself at a fast food restaurant taking orders. I liked the people that I worked with so it wasn't so bad, I mean, apart from the endless grease and hateful customers. I've often joked about bad service at fast food restaurants, but trust me there can be clueless slackjaws on both sides of the counter.

If you don't think restaurant patrons would test the patience of Job, then you've never worked in one. Really, Mr. Irregular, just because the bathroom stall is closed doesn't mean you can make that solid deposit in the urinal. I think the real reason for those tiny little widows at the drive-thru is so nobody gets hurt when drunks come through that call you names. The insanity just goes on and on. I did so grow to miss computers.

A particularly special memory was when I was accosted by a jealous lover of another employee looking for a fight. He loudly asked if I was the person he was looking for and called them by name. Now you should know, personalized ball caps were big at the time, and I was wearing one with my name embroidered on the front of it.

In a here's your sign moment, I raised my hand slowly and pointed to the name on my cap. Through clenched teeth, I said, "Does this look like it says who you're looking for?"

Like the circulating joke goes, "I used to be a people person, but people ruined that for me." Needless to say I was eager to go back to school.

Profit isn't always money. Sometimes it's experience.

> "All hard work brings a profit, but mere talk leads only to poverty." (Proverbs 14:23 NIV)

• Dating anxiety can be horrific. Forgetting how to make words come out of your mouth tends to make impressing a girl so much more difficult, and that's just when you're mustering the nerve to ask them out for the first time.

If you were brimming with confidence with the opposite sex even on first dates, then I salute you. In the beginning at least, most of us just try to cover up our awkwardness as best we can and blunder through them. Especially everyone's very first date.

There was a nice girl that I was friends with in high school that was cute and fun to be around. I found the courage to ask her out, and the movies seemed like a safe bet. No need to struggle with communication. Just be entertained by the show.

Wrong. Stupid car ride. Seems you have to fill them with conversation. Normally talking and laughing friends, I quickly discovered that a date somehow made it different. More pressured. Gorillas probably communicate more coherently than I did with her, but I was the guy so somehow I was supposed to know what I was doing. Completely wrong.

Suddenly every personal detail is under your own scrutiny. You find yourself wondering if your deodorant has given out, whether or not she heard your stomach growl, and if you remembered to check your zipper.

We made it through a burger and a show. After a bunch of words probably put together in no particular order during the ride home, our date finally came to a close. Of course, I parked the passenger side so close to a bush at her mother's house that she needed hedge clippers to make it to her front door. Oh, I was a smooth operator.

> "The Lord God said, 'It is not good for the man to be alone. I will make a helper suitable for him,'" (Genesis 2:18 NIV) Nobody said finding the right helper would be easy.

We remained friends, but we didn't go on anymore dates. Crazy as it sounds, I'm grateful for the memory. Reflecting on this, I know every experience didn't have to turn out perfectly because God had another helper in mind for me.

Chapter XIII

LISA AND THE LIBRARY

Working at a hospital, I had the occasion to see a covered gurney being rolled to the back of an extra long Cadillac. Not the most pleasant way to start a day, but there was a soft voice somewhere behind this scene asking, "What's your excuse for not making the best of today?"

Not sky diving or climbing mountains. Not trips to Paris or spa pampering. None of that kind of thing matters in the end.

Tell someone what they mean to you. Better yet, go out of your way to show them. Break your routine for who is on your heart. Let go and forgive. Dare to love.

Be moved by God.

One man's journey was done. He could try no more, but you still have the opportunity to be salt and light. Unless the door has closed on your last ride, then there is really no excuse for not making the best of today.

- When I first learned of Hell as a youth, it wasn't dressed up or watered down: hell is a place of burning torment where those who make a final refusal of Jesus are going.

The world easily accepts a Heaven based on merit, yet rejects a Hell based on the same. They are wrong on both counts, because the Word teaches that there are none righteous and salvation is a gift.

No one is getting into Heaven by being good enough. Without God, we are rotten at the core and bound for Hell.

His holy nature could not allow sin to go unpunished, but Hell alone does not break a sinner's heart. God does not win sons and daughters by threat. He wins them by love!

In love he took the cross. Not just to make an escape from condemnation, but so we could be accepted as his own!

Never underestimate the value of telling people there is a Hell.

- This is a short fictional story that I found wandering in my heart, and I needed to give it a home:

Lisa hadn't noticed the man that had come to the periodicals section until the sound of a hard case made an obnoxious thud on the table only a few feet away from her.

"May I sit here?" asked the man who was already getting his laptop out.

"Sure," she answered, now taking the time to examine the library's latest visitor.

Right away, she felt he was out of place because of his clothes that seemed more appropriate for the pulpit rather than a country library. A red silk tie pointed to a face that was ridiculously handsome. Jet black hair and a manicured beard that was short and tight finished the look that could have been cut from one of the fashion magazines laying nearby. She wanted to stare, but forced herself to turn her attention back to her college journalism project, satisfying herself with the thought that he was far too old for her.

"The internet connection here is terrible, but business can't always wait," he said as he settled into the chair directly across from her. Lisa acknowledged him with a nod. Uncomfortable with the idea of a conversation starting, she went back to one of the many newspapers sprawled out in front of her.

The headlines were sickening. Each story tried to top the last with injustice and suffering. Then there was politics. Oh how she hated politics! Everyone had one thing in common no matter their party, and that was the feeling the other side was lying.

"Some of my finest work in politics. Divide and conquer," came from the man as a grin spread across his face without looking up from his typing.

"Excuse me?" Lisa now felt more awkward with her uninvited neighbor. He couldn't possibly have known exactly what she was reading. His eyes were fixed on the screen, but didn't seem to follow his work. Instead, his gaze was holding something unseen by Lisa, and the gleam in his eyes couldn't have come from the florescent lights overhead.

"The last election turned out better than I hoped. The fact is, I don't even care anymore which side wins. I'm going to win." His last statement seemed to hang almost tangibly in the air between them, and she wanted to leave but she was paralyzed with the idea she shouldn't turn her back to him.

"What do you mean?" she managed to ask, but not really wanting to know.

"It's simple really. Right. Left. Both are caught in the middle of much bigger fight. I'm winning, because neither side is paying attention to the crux of their problems." Things seemed out of focus past the two of them now, like being enclosed in a bubble of opaque glass. "Some serve me more than others, though most don't even believe in me. Even those claiming to oppose me think they can stand against me in their own strength." A laugh from him brought a wave of nausea.

Closing the lid of the laptop, his eyes now clearly rested on her. "I've been doing a little research on the internet. As it turns out, the voice that can make a difference in the outcome that matters to me...is you."

Tears began trailing down Lisa's cheeks. Fear held her tongue and legs in a way she'd never known.

"What's wrong? Things are going to get worse, but you don't have to worry. You're a smart girl, you read the news, so you surely realize by now God doesn't care or things wouldn't be this shape. You just focus on you, and I'll take care of the rest. You won't have to suffer with all these other losers. Raising your voice for Him is just a waste of time. Either way, I'll get what I want. However, if you'll be quiet and let it happen, then I can get what I want so much faster. Maybe I'll even score a few extra points, and in return I'll make sure you are very comfortable." His smile would have been charming except for the realization of who was before her.

"Lisa?" A touch on her shoulder from behind became a conduit of panic. Startled by the contact, she jerked her head from her resting arms that had been folded in front on the table. "Lisa, are you okay?" The elderly frame of Mrs. Stanford, one of the librarians, was bent to her side. "I came to this corner to straighten the magazines before we closed, and I noticed you here sleeping." She was relieved to see an empty chair in front of her.

Reaching up a little, she gave Mrs. Stanford a hug. Gratitude for all those Sunday school lessons she taught her when she was little welled to the surface, "I'm so glad you found me. I'd have hated to get trapped in here."

Gathering up her things took half the time it normally would. "No more staying up all night," she said to herself. All the other patrons had gone for the day so the front parking area was empty save for her car as she made her way to it. Standing beside the car door digging for keys in her tote, the unusual hum of a hot rod engine made her turn to look. It was a very nice sports car, but she didn't know cars well enough to identify it. Certainly too high class for the residents of her town. She intentionally dug around a few extra seconds hoping to get a better look.

Time seemed to slow as the driver clearly turned to Lisa as he went by. A red tie pointed to an unmistakable face. A wink from him froze the image indelibly in her mind. She watched the car until it ran the stop sign at the end of the street before turning the corner and going out of sight.

Lisa remembered his offer. There was nothing in it to compare to the love she first came to realize in Mrs. Stanford's class. She decided it had been entirely too long since the last time she'd prayed. The ride home would be a good place to start.

Chapter XIV

HERE IN THIS MOMENT

Toy aisles are lined with them. Plastic dolls with perfect expressions. Just the right clothes. Each one exactly like the one behind it and very much like the one beside it. All designed to warm a little girl's heart, but empty on the inside.

How many churches are like the dolls on those toy aisles, full of people trying to act exactly as those around them expect, but not really focusing on God? Wanting to appear just right so they won't be taken for less than the ones beside them, but empty on the inside because they never really invite him?

I wonder these things, but I'm not looking at them in a position of judgment. You see, there was a time that I was sitting on the shelf in a box beside my neighbors. After all, if they've got it all figured out, then by now I should too. I looked around at everyone else in church, so I knew how to act: as if everything was wonderful and my faith was perfect. God forgive me, but that wasn't true.

Shallow pools in the South quickly become stagnant if they don't have clean water flowing into them, and I was a shallow pool with no flow. By only producing the expectations of those around me, nothing was happening. Then I began to refocus on the reality of Jesus and things began to change.

"The next day Jesus decided to leave for Galilee. Finding Philip, he said to him, 'Follow me.'" (John 1:43 NIV) The Bible doesn't go into precisely how much Philip knew of Jesus when the Lord asked him to follow. Certainly enough that he did, as he quickly revealed to another who he believed Jesus to be. There was no long explanation of why following outweighed Philip going along with his life as it had been, so one was not necessary. His command was simple, "Follow me."

Hurtful distractions are everywhere. Some may be well intended, so it is important to notice he was not asked to follow along with the crowd that often followed Jesus.

A risk exists of a person being misleading no matter how good their intentions may be. Pastors, preachers, and Bible speakers are all men subject to error, just like you and me. It does not matter if they've been in the ministry field all their lives with a mountain of good works to their credit. They too can find themselves on the shelf. If they're not genuinely operating under God's calling or are promoting a new god that's more acceptive of the world as it wants to be, then they can't lead anyone in the right direction.

You can recognize the dangers by building your relationship with Christ! Make time to pray. Read the Bible, not just a book that touches it. Discernment of the truth comes from the Word. Not that books and givers of the Gospel can't be great, but just because the image of a cross is on something doesn't make it holy.

"Follow me," is our command, not "Stay in the box."

- It was the weekend and my family was trying its best to sleep late on Saturday morning. Although our little inside dog tried to tell us something was wrong, his barking was quickly hushed by us in the hope of catching up on much needed rest. Later, I would even remember hearing an engine deep in the night, but had dismissed it thinking someone was riding an ATV on our fence line or in the nearby pasture.

Fatigue makes a great pillow, but pain makes a lousy mattress. I tried really hard to sleep longer than my spouse, but the older I get the less I am able to just lay in the bed. My body won't let me do it indefinitely whether I feel rested or not.

So putting on my pants to let the dog out and stepping to the edge of my carport, I was surprised to see a truck with the front end against an oak tree in my yard. It was so out of place that I stood there a moment not believing. It may as well have been an alien spacecraft because the fog hadn't quite lifted from my consciousness.

The rut around their rear tires and the dirt that had been thrown backwards indicated that they'd tried to go forward after coming to rest against the tree. I knew there had been a party down the street the night before so I was somewhat sure of the cause of what I was seeing. Alcohol had dulled this person's senses to the point that they did not know what they were doing.

I picked up the dog and went back inside for my shoes. By the time I got back outside the drunk that had been passed out on the front seat awakened and managed to get his truck rolling down the driveway. I tried to wave him down and shouted for him to stop. However, the little nap he had while parked out by my bird bath worked wonders for restoring his determination to drive. I'm not defending him, but I'm not sure I'd have wanted to have stopped for a conversation with an upset, bed headed, shirtless man holding a pistol either.

After reporting it to the police, I discovered in the following week who it was from them. They said I could press charges against him for any property damages if I wanted. The tree would be fine and I'd already filled the rut back, but I was worried that there would be another incident with far more disastrous results.

He asked through the police if I would be willing to speak with him, and I was. The young man apologized and offered to make restitution, but I told him there wasn't anything that he needed to repay me. Thankfully, serious damage wasn't involved so there was no need for civil restitution. I asked him if he went to church, and he told me where he went. I told him if he'd go to church that Sunday that he could consider us even.

He needed forgiveness, but not from me.

There is no shortage of people that would have looked on what had happened as an opportunity for personal gain, but the gain we should want most isn't from people, "Blessed are the merciful, for they will be shown mercy." (Matthew 5:7 NIV)

- Too young and wanting to be with friends who were swimmers led me in the water toward a floating deck on an Ozark lake. A wrong step made me realize I was in over my head. Not yet able to swim, I panicked as the murky water closed over me. As I struggled to find the bottom I breathed in thinking my head had broken the surface only to find it hadn't. I was flailing in desperation. In an instant I became afraid that I was about to die. Then my toes found the bottom. Coughing and sputtering, I made my way to the beach. No one had even noticed.

God noticed.

A few years later while spending time with a cousin at his grandmother's house out in the country found me in mischief. We'd decided to make a game of breaking bottles on the side of the road and make the tiny pieces rain into the steep ditch nearby. He broke one while I was in the ditch looking for another. Bad judgment sent the bottom of the broken bottle directly into my neck. I held a denim jacket on the wound on the way to the hospital. The jugular vein was visible, but it escaped harm from the glass. Millimeters were the difference between simple stitches and bleeding out on a roadside.

God measured the difference.

Then there was the time I'd rode my motorcycle to visit my dad who'd recently divorced my mom. It wasn't street legal, but I didn't really care. Sand on a horseshoe road made the rear wheel slide out from under me when I leaned into the curve. Going off the shoulder sent me over the handlebars and slammed my leg into the ground. My knee would be scarred, but I would be okay.

God knew all my scars, even those that couldn't be seen that had me on that road in the first place.

My point is that I've been in situations where the hereafter was separated perhaps by the thickness of the paper on which God has written my appointed time. He put my feet back on solid ground when I could have drowned. He kept the jagged glass from a fatal mark. He limited the wreck to be no more than a scar.

My mortal existence has been spared to teach me his grace, and through his grace to learn my part for his kingdom. Apparently, I'm a slow learner, but I've learned that I need to tell and show others what I believe.

The price Jesus paid for my sins was too great to be taken for granted, and what he has given me should not return void.

I'm grateful God has saved me, body and soul. He brought me through all those times so I could be in this moment with his purpose for me. I want to be the person that he saw I could become all those times, and I want to bring friends to him.

Chapter XV

Chewing Tobacco

Jury duty is a civic responsibility that everyone should respect. Those who complain about it will be the very ones protected by it should they ever stand wrongfully accused. After my name appeared on a list for petit jury, I prayed God's will in the outcome of the selection.

Never having experienced being a juror left me curious about the process, and I knew I had no legitimate reason to ask to be excused. I would not be there for the prosecution or the defense. I would be there for what was right. God expects that of us–in all circumstances. "He hath shewed thee, O man, what is good; and what doth the Lord require of thee, but to do justly, and to love mercy, and to walk humbly with thy God?" (Micah 6:8 KJV)

Chewing Tobacco

Spectators and potential jurors sat together in court as the selection process began. It was easy to feel sympathy for the candidates being questioned because I knew how public speaking is a massive fear for many. I didn't always grasp the reasoning behind the questions, but I knew it was so both sides could be satisfied with their ability to impartially serve.

It was easy to sense the necessity of the process sitting in the courtroom. You could tell some spectators had already passed judgment–on the potential jurors! From the murmurs of some, I'm not sure it would have mattered if the seats had been filled with Moses and the original apostles, you couldn't have made them happy. As much as love is blind to imperfection, hatred is blind to virtue.

Somewhere between someone lacking in personal hygiene and another trying to cough up a lung, the first day came to a close. No jury had been seated, so it would be at least another day.

My name was drawn the second day to replace others who were excused. Holding a microphone and answering personal questions from attorneys was all the fun an overdue trip to the dentist. I went from staring to being stared.

Finally, it came to the alternate juror's seat and I was the last candidate from the second group to be decided upon. I remembered my prayer. Selected or not, I could be satisfied that it was God's will.

I'll never know their reasons for picking me, but I found a jury assembly room full of good people. There was a willingness to welcome the Lord's guidance in our duty from the very first day.

A day is fast approaching when we will all find ourselves in a heavenly courtroom. We will each be on trial for our lives, and the judge will have perfect discernment. Be prepared with the only acceptable defense, "But God demonstrates his own love for us in this: While we were still sinners, Christ died for us." (Romans 5:8 NIV)

- I've had a certain paperweight since I was a young boy. There is nothing valuable about the stones of which it is made and nothing terribly creative about how it is put together. It's nothing anyone would count by its appearance as being anything other than silly. Today, as I look at it, I know that I would not trade it for its weight in gold. On the occasion of my baptism, my grandma Hightower gave me this little paperweight. It was purchased from a gift shop in the hospital where she'd recently had to stay.

She revered joining the family of God, and wanted to give me a gift to help remember the day. She was sick–no one could have found fault in her for staying home. There were so many things going on then, a small gesture surely wouldn't matter.

But it did matter. Grandma Hightower made me feel loved. I've heard it said that memories may fade, but you will never forget how someone made you feel. She came to my baptismal service in a wheelchair because it was important to her. I was important to her, not only as her grandson, but she was moving in her role in the body of Christ.

Jesus said, "Let the little children come to me, and do not hinder them, for the kingdom of God belongs to such as these." (partial Luke 18:16 NIV) In John we read, "Yet to all who did receive him, to those who believed in his name, he gave the right to become children of God." (John 1:12 NIV) By his word, I was welcomed.

If only I'd been as unchanging in faith since that day as the unchanging stone from which this token was made.

This paperweight has done a better job of living up to what it was meant to be than me. I've abused God's grace and done things that make me grimace to recollect. Doubt and fear entered my life as I grew older that I wish had never found a foothold to grow.

Still, I find myself wanting to draw nearer to God than ever before. The same Spirit that moved my grandma to give this paperweight so long ago reaches across time and says, "I still want you to be mine just as I did then."

Where ever you've strayed, he still wants you to be his. You don't have to think of yourself as being defined as the sum of all your mistakes, but as a child of the King. Go back to him.

> "...But while he was still a long way off, his father saw him and was filled with compassion for him; he ran to his son, threw his arms around him and kissed him." (partial Luke 15:20 NIV)

Chewing Tobacco

- The local fair was in town, and I was there with my crazy friends. In your teenage years it's like a right of passage to deny your common sense and ride the scariest things possible. It didn't matter that the men putting them together looked like derelicts you'd find around a 17th century ship dock. Running with the pack overruled any fear of parts forgotten in the assembly of machines that were inspired by the nightmares of clowns.

Managing to temporarily put girls on a back burner long enough to enjoy the rides, we rode everything we could. The Hurl-o-tron, the Vominator, and the Octo-barfer: those names weren't the real ones, but they made conquering them a lot more fun.

All that excitement makes a young man hungry, so lucky for us all the junk food shacks were there. Judging by the trailers vending the deep fried delicacies, sanitizing was accomplished by occasionally wiping them down with the leftover grease. That didn't stop us from loading up on funnel cakes and sausage on a stick.

After a fast paced evening of spending my parent's hard earned money, I hadn't quite satisfied my need for mischief. Thank goodness for friends that had that covered.

Out came the chewing tobacco. Far be it from me to use my brain at that point. Even though I knew my mother wouldn't approve of what I was doing, I let the sugar and adrenaline coursing through my veins chose for me. The funny thing about breaking commandments is that they don't actually break–we do.

Slamming myself against honoring my parents, the thick syrupy sweet leaves began to make my head spin. This would be the banner of proof that I was man enough to handle anything. I was invincible!

Well, in about five minutes the invincibility wore off. I might have survived rides and fair food, but I was laid low by tobacco. Greener than the grass I was leaning over, the error of my ways came back to me. So did the sausage on a stick, funnel cake, and everything I must have eaten in the last week.

Once the buzz was gone and all my tanks were empty, I still had to declare it a successful evening with my friends. It's true that a lot of good judgment comes from experience, and a lot of experience comes from poor judgment.

"Do not remember the sins of my youth and my rebellious ways; according to your love remember me, for you, Lord, are good." (Psalms 25:7 NIV)

Chapter XVI

Perfect

I am not the most emotional person in the world. One of the things that I find beautiful about my wife is the depth in which she feels the things that she does. Maybe it's natural that being at opposite ends of the emotional spectrum would draw us together. Yet, while I admire that aspect of her, she doesn't like that her emotions are sometimes difficult to restrain.

On the other hand, I've often looked at others and wondered why I didn't seem to be as overtaken by my feelings as the people around me. There would be a sense of what I should be feeling, but I thought there might be something wrong with me because my reaction didn't seem to measure up.

Perfect

The more I've sought Jesus in my life, the less I've beat myself up about it, and interestingly enough, the more easily moved my heart has become. Granted, there are days that I don't feel very spiritual, but there have also been times that my voice has broken in merely speaking his name. My friends, that is welcome change.

So, whatever it is you're dealing with inside, be encouraged, because we are all works in progress! The breath you exhale in prayer marks the beginning of your healing.

We may differ in our shortcomings, but we share the same need for a savior. God is faithful in his mercy, and if you need a new beginning then, "Humble yourselves before the Lord, and he will lift you up." (James 4:10 NIV)

- We used to have an outdoor swing set that I had to work around. While I would be busy in the yard on the riding mower, my little boy would be swinging by himself and hoping for a little attention. As I circled around him cutting the grass, he didn't always know I was watching him, but every now and then, I would stop right in front of him until he looked up.

Then I would pretend to be taking his picture. His face would light up with a smile and a laugh.

I just made the motions with my hands. I had no camera, but clarity of those moments are perfectly preserved in my heart. Being a parent has given me greater understanding of how God must look at us.

In our lives as his children, I think sometimes we're on that swing. Maybe we feel God is to busy for us, but the truth is he is always keeping a careful eye on us. We crave our heavenly daddy's attention, and he lights up our faces when we recognize the blessings he prepared with his own hands.

Maybe at some point you feel a little lonely sitting on the swing all by yourself, but be encouraged because the time is coming when everything is right, that he's going to come over and give you the push you need. You are not forgotten.

> "For I am convinced that neither death nor life, neither angels nor demons, neither the present nor the future, nor any powers, neither height nor depth, nor

anything else in all creation, will be able to separate us from the love of God that is in Christ Jesus our Lord." (Romans 8:38-39 NIV)

- The first payday of the new year was hopefully a deeper revelation to some about where we're going as a nation. Seeing the increased taxes and cost of benefits was as pleasant as being asked to chew up a red worm. This morning, as I sat and watched the price of fuel rolling up before my eyes at the gas station, I practically tingled with confidence that America is on the right track. It's just been blow after blow lately.

The failure of our leaders to deliver a better future to everyone is, in all honesty, too big for them alone. We can't expect a rally of the the principles of our founding fathers when the enemies of those principles have been allowed to subjugate so many. Things look dark on the horizon, but no one has to be afraid. God is still on the throne.

While I listened to people talk about the hit in their paycheck, the story of Peter telling the collectors of the temple tax that Jesus would pay came to mind.

The tax collectors asked him if Jesus paid the temple tax, and before he was even sure of the situation, he told them the Lord would. When Peter approached Jesus, the Lord asked, "From whom do the kings of the earth collect duty and taxes, from their own children or from others?" Peter answered others.

The Lord was pointing out that a ruler's children are exempt from such demands. Peter no longer belonged to them, but was a child of God so he could expect to pay their taxes.

The flip side of that is as a child of God, we are exempt from the price that will be demanded of sin. One day, everyone will be called into account for themselves, and no earthly stature or statute will matter. Only the presence of the blood of Christ in our hearts will cover it.

Pay attention to the ending of this story too. To keep the peace with the temple tax collectors, Peter was instructed to go fishing. More than a few of us would be happy to accept being told to go to Caney Lake when faced with a problem! The Lord told him the first fish he caught would have a coin in its mouth to pay the tax for both of them. I wish I could have seen him catch it. Had he not done it, there would have been no coin. It's clear by moving in faith, his children will be given what they need. (see Matthew 17:24-27)

Don't give up! If we move forward in faith, then we don't have to be afraid.

• Give or take a few words, this is my testimony that I shared at church one morning:

My wife would probably say you are seeing a miracle. Let's just say the distance between pew and podium has proved to be a lot further than it looks, particularly for someone like me. Call it pride, call it fear, I've remarked many times that I'd rather take a beating than stand before a crowd. Right now, I'm as far out of my comfort zone as I can get.

I've heard beautiful testimonies of lives radically changed from overtly sinful to lives of faith. Like so many that grew up in church, I haven't felt that I had a testimony particularly worth sharing. I was baptized when I was eight years old at the First Baptist Church of Dodson. Forgiveness and eternal life sounded sweet, and when Jesus said, "Let the little children come to me," I took him up on the offer.

Then something happened. As I matured, so did my understanding of what it means to believe. I knew I needed to be willing to do whatever God would have of me. I asked myself, "What if God wants me to speak for him," and I pushed away. Thankfully, the Holy Spirit didn't let go. There was no blinding light on the way to Damascus, but I can take you to the moment and place it happened, and I was walking on a road.

I've been struggling with it for a very long time. On one hand, I can't deny my earthly insecurities, prideful though they've been. But on the other, willingness to act in spite of them is part of what belief really is. Proving that willingness to myself is why I'm standing before you.

Moses offered up excuses in Exodus for his self perceived weakness saying, "Pardon your servant, Lord. I have never been eloquent, neither in the past nor since you have spoken to your servant. I am slow of speech and tongue." He wanted God to send someone else. I've basically made the same kind of excuse saying, "Lord, I'm more at home in a cave than a crowd. Possibly under a rock. Speaking in front of people just isn't me." But maybe that's the point–it isn't me.

Lately, I've enjoyed devotional writing, but the truth is, I'm not sure that it is what he would have of me. It would be easy to accept the suggestion that my service to him be something I enjoy, but I want to lay any unwillingness down so that he might draw closer. I've been praying he take my fear. I need his encouragement and design on my life, and I know I don't want to go on as a spiritually crippled Christian.

My fears, my inadequacies, are what I hope he will draw me beyond because in Corinthians it is recorded, "My grace is sufficient for you, for my power is made perfect in weakness."

I'm not self confident standing here. I'm not pretending any wisdom of my own. I just want to know that I am his. And I'm realizing he is saying, "Perfect."

Epilogue:

When my children were little, I wrote this prayer to share with them at bedtime. I tried to use language that they could understand, but the spirit of it is something meant for everyone, and I hope they see it in me. As you part company with me from these pages I want to share it with you:

Heavenly Father,

Thank you for this day and all the good things in it. You never forget us, but always hold us in your heart. When we are sad, we know you are sad too and will ease our sorrow. We thank you for caring for us in ways we may not see. Even though we may not understand why bad things happen,

Epilogue:

we know you never stop loving us and will help us go on.

Help us do the things that please you, and use our lives to help those around us. Encourage us to do what is right by moving on our hearts. We are committed to living as you would have us live, and will do whatever you would have of us. You know and want what is best for us.

Bless those that we hold dear in our hearts. Bless those who don't like us, because we hope they will become our friends. Provide us with the things we need, and make our happy moments greater than our sad.

Please forgive us of our sins. We believe you died on the cross to make this possible for us. Not only do you forgive us, but you give us the promise of heaven, and that gives us something to look forward to no matter what happens to us.

Continue to show your love to us, and have mercy on us when we are not as we should be.

In the name of Jesus we ask these things.

Amen.

ABOUT ME:

I've worked in the health care industry for many years as a clinical data analyst. I have two degrees from Louisiana Tech University, one in business and one in health information. My wife and two children are extensions of my very life and are blessings beyond price. Despite all the blessings, I didn't feel that I had much in my life worth talking about that would serve God.

This work is part of my own discovery of the satisfaction of sharing testimony and truth.

I'm not a preacher, but I am impelled to stand for the gospel. I never taught Sunday school, but I want to share what I know. Sometimes I don't even feel like I'm a very good Christian, but being Christian is not about your feelings in the moment–it's about being committed to the truth.

What is the gospel? Gospel means "good news." The good news is that God loved you so much that he came from heaven to make a way for you to be with him. Jesus is that way.

What do I know? Jesus came not as a majestic earthly king wielding a mighty sword, but as a humble servant wielding a mighty word. He gave his perfect life to restore the lives we taint with sin. No sin can withstand the cleansing flow of his blood shed at the cross. We have only to submit them.

What is truth? Truth is not about some grand philosophy designed by the hearts of men. It is not about how good we feel as the result of blessings or how bad we feel from their absence. It is not about demonstrating the things counted as the nobler side of human nature. The truth every man needs to know about is a person, and that person is Jesus Christ.

I hope everyone connecting with me has the everlasting life God wants to give them. He desperately desires to be your heavenly father. Let today be the day you invite him into your heart and life by prayer, "For he says, 'In the time of my favor I heard you, and in the day

About me:

of salvation I helped you.' I tell you, now is the time of God's favor, now is the day of salvation." (2 Corinthians 6:2 NIV)